KB194709

NEW
SMART

다시영 다시 시작하는 영어

영어회화는 동사싸움이다!

|구동사편| CHRIS SUH

MENT⊘RS

다시영 구동사편

영어회화는 동사싸움이다!

2025년 03월 04일 인쇄
2025년 03월 11일 발행

지 은 이 Chris Suh
발 행 인 Chris Suh
발 행 처 **MENT☺RS**
　　　　　 경기도 성남시 분당구 황새울로 335번길 10 598
　　　　　 TEL 031-604-0025 FAX 031-696-5221
　　　　　 mentors.co.kr
　　　　　 blog.naver.com/mentorsbook
　　　　　 * Play 스토어 및 App 스토어에서 '멘토스북' 검색해 어플다운받기!
등록일자 2005년 7월 27일
등록번호 제 2009-000027호
I S B N   979-11-94467-55-7
가　 격　 15,600원

잘못 인쇄된 책은 교환해 드립니다.
이 책에 게재된 내용의 일부 또는 전체를 무단으로 복제 및 발췌하는 것을 금합니다.

네이티브들의 유별난 동사사랑~

네이티브들은 쉬운 단어로 영어를 자유자재로 한다. 그 쉬운 단어에서 핵심은 뭐니뭐니 해도 기본동사이다. 요즘은 많이 좋아졌지만 어려운 관용어구 및 우리가 안써도 되는 슬랭을 많이 알고 있는 것을 영어잘하는 것으로 착각하는 시절이 있었다. 막상 네이티브와 만나게 되면 영어로 인사 몇 마디 나누고서 할 말이 없어서 꿀먹은 벙어리가 되는 경우가 허다하다. 특히 기본동사 중에서도 네이티브들이 좋아하는 것은 동사구이다. 어떻게 보면 한 단어로 말하면 되는 것을 두 단어 이상으로 하니까 비효율적으로 보일 수도 있지만, 쉬운 단어들로만 구성된다는 점에서 이해가 된다. 예를 들어 examine보다는 go over를 visit 보다는 come over, drop by, look up, 그리고 separate보다 는 break up with나 split up 등을 즐겨 사용한다.

네이티브는 어려운 단어를 잘 안써!

영어도 하나의 언어이다보니 어려운 것보다는 쉽고 편한 쪽으로 가려는 습성이 무척 강하다. 따라서 기본적이기는 하지만 네이티브가 가장 많이 쓰는 동사구들을 완벽하게 자기 것으로 만드는 것은 자신의 영어 말하기 실력을 올리는 가장 최선의 선택일 것이다. 낯설다고 어렵다고 푸념하지 말고 반복학습해야 한다. 또한 스스로 안다고 생각했지만 막상 쓰지 못하는 표현들을 제대로 실전에서 쓰게끔 실전연습해야 영어회화의 큰 고비를 넘길 수 있을 것이다.

영어는 동사싸움이다!

〈영어회화는 동사싸움이다!〉는 이런 관점에서 네이티브들이 시도때도 없이 쓰는 동사구를 전치사별로 수록하였다. 전치사별로 수록한 이유는 전치사의 개념을 조금 알게 되면 〈동사+전치사〉의 동사구 의미를 몰라도 어느 정도 유추할 수 있기 때문이다. 상대방 쪽으로(over) 가니까(come) come over하게 되면 들르다, 방문하다가 되고, 다음의 관심사항으로(on) 이동하다(move)가 되는 move on은 지금 하는 일에서 다음 일로 넘어가거나 혹은 비유적으로 안좋은 일을 잊고 가다로 쓰이기도 한다. 그리고 밑에(down) 내려놓다(put)라는 put down은 글자 그대로 뭔가를 바닥이나 밑에 내려놓거나, 기록하거나, 전화를 끊거나 혹은 비유적으로 진압하거나 비난하다라는 의미로 발전한다. 따라서 중요한 것은 전치사와 동사의 의미를 잘 새겨서 의미를 연상해보는 상상력을 발휘하는게 맹목적으로 외우는 것보다 훨씬 더 효율적인 학습방법이 될 것이다. 이런 쉬운 단어들로 구성된 동사구를 자유자재로 구사하게 되어 다양한 문장을 만들다 보면 나도 모르게 네이티브들처럼 쉬운 단어들로 영어회화를 하는 자신을 발견하게 될 것이다.

1️⃣ 실제 네이티브들이 즐겨 쓰는 동사구 500 여개를 수록하였다.

2️⃣ 쉬운 영어로 설명하여 각 동사구를 감각적으로 익힐 수 있도록 기획되었다.

3️⃣ 예문 2개로 동사구가 어떻게 쓰이는지 두 눈과 두 귀로 확인한다.

4️⃣ 다음 생생한 다이알로그를 통해 동사구의 실전 사용법을 몸으로 익힌다.

5️⃣ 모든 영문은 네이티브의 녹음이 들어있어 실감나게 역동적으로 학습할 수 있다.

1️⃣ 수록표현

네이티브들이 가장 많이 사용하는 동사구 500여개를 Unit01-06까지 전치사별로 구분 정리하였다.

2️⃣ Unit 01 ~ 07

Unit 01 in, out이 만들어내는 동사구

Unit 02 up, down이 만들어내는 동사구

Unit 03 for, of, on이 만들어내는 동사구

Unit 04 to, with, about이 만들어내는 동사구

Unit 05 over, off, back, from, at이 만들어내는 동사구

Unit 06 away~ through가 만들어내는 동사구

Unit 07 동사별 총정리: 수록한 동사구를 전치사가 아니라 동사별로 구분 정리하였다.

영어는 동사싸움이다! 이렇게 보면 된다

❶ 동사구 엔트리

❷ 영영/의미/보충
동사구의 영영설명과 우리말 의미 그리고 보충설명이 이어진다.

❸ 예문
예문 2개로 동사구의 쓰임새를 확인한다.

❹ 다이알로그
동사구가 쓰인 다이알로그를 통해서 실제로 동사구의 쓰임새를 파악한다.

❶ 동사별 총정리
이번에는 동사별로 정리한 동사구 리스트. 새로운 각도에서 머리속에 정리하자는 말씀!

Unit 01 **in·out**   019

work in …에서 일하다
turn in 제출하다, 잠자리에 들다
take in 섭취하다, 옷줄이다, 속이다, 집에 머물게 하다
drop in 잠깐 들르다
check in 체크인하다, 확인하다, (SNS) 어디있는지 알리다
check in on 확인하다
bring in 가지고 오다, 영입하다, 도입하다
believe in …의 존재를 믿다, …가 맞다고 믿다
engage in 특정한 행위를 하다
major in 전공하다
hand in 제출하다
give in 포기하다, 제출하다
stay in 장시간 머물다, 어떤 상태를 계속 유지하다
break in 불법침입하다, (구두) 길들이다, 새로운 연장, 도구를 쓰다
fill in 서류작성을 하다, 세부사항을 말해주다, 대신 일봐주다
enroll in 수강하러 등록하다, 가입하다
keep in 억제하다, 감추다, 못나가게 하다
join in 함께 하다
step in 개입하다
spend in 시간과 돈을 보내다
count sb in 포함시키다
run in (one's family) 집안 내력이다
put in 시간이나 노력을 기울이다
put in for 공식적으로 요청하다, 신청하다
go in for 즐기다, 열중하다
fall in with 어울리다, 생각을 받아들이다
get involved in 연루되다, 사귀다
take part in 참여하다
pay in cash 현금으로 계산하다
take pride in 자부심을 느끼다
get in touch with 연락을 취하다

be into   관심갖다, 푹 빠져있다

get into   …하기 시작하다, …에 빠지다

go into   …에 들어가다, 상세히 설명하다

check into   조사하다, 체크인하다

run into   우연히 만나다

bump into   우연히 만나다

look into   조사하다, 안을 자세히 보다

turn into   …이 되다, 방향을 바꾸다

fall into   …한 상태가 되다, 계획에 없던 일을 시작하다

tap into   두드리다, 접근하다, 자료를 얻다

sneak into   몰래 들어가다

break into   침입하다, …하기 시작하다, 새로운 분야에 뛰어들다

talk sb into   설득해서 …하게 하다

look out   조심하다

hang out   어울리다, 몸을 내밀다

find out   정보 등을 알아내다

check out   확인하다, 체크아웃하다, 계산하다, 책빌리다

give out   정지하다, 배포하다, (빛) 발하다

move out   이사가다

leave out   제외하다, 밖에 두다

break out   도망가다, (종기) 나다, 발발하다

pick out   선택하다, 제외시키다

see out   (문밖에서) 배웅하다

help out   도와주다

hand out   나눠주다, 정보를 건네다

stand out   두드러지다

fill out   서류작성하다, 살이 찌다

point out   지적하다, 언급하다, 가리키다

work out   잘되다, 운동하다, 해결하다

figure out   이해하다, 해결책을 알아내다

watch out   주의하다, 조심하다

ask out   데이트신청하다

make out   이해하다, 알아보다, 성공하다, 애정행위하다

hold out   굴복하지 않다, 희망하다

burn out   완전히 지치다

set out   시작하다, 물건을 밖에 두다

take out 꺼내다, 데리고 나가다, 제거하다
turn out 모습을 드러내다, 드러나다
pass out 졸도하다, 의식을 잃다
black out 의식잃다, 정전되다
stress out 스트레스를 주다
win out 이기다, 승리하다
eat out 외식하다
blow out 불어 끄다, 쉽게 이기다, 펑크나다, 큰 파티를 열다
sell out 다 팔다, 신념을 버리다
chew out 호되게 꾸짖다, 야단치다
keep out 들여보내지 않다
hear out 끝까지 듣다
freak out 질겁하다, 화나다
get out 나가다
go out 나가다, 외출하다, (전기) 꺼지다
drop out 학교 등을 그만두다
come out 나오다, 게이임을 밝히다
stay out of 안좋은 일에 끼지 않다
grow out of (습관) 그만두다, …에서 생기다, 커서 옷이 안맞다
sneak out 몰래 빠져나가다
take sb out of 설득하여 …하지 못하게 하다
miss out on 좋은 기회를 놓치다

Unit 02 **up·down** 065

get up 일어나다, 잠에서 깨다
show up 모임 장소에 나오다, 당황하게 하다
cheer up 기운나게 하다
give up 포기하다
hurry up 서두르다
bring up 양육하다, 화제를 꺼내다, 컴퓨터 화면에 띄우다
grow up 성장하다, 자라서 …가 되다
pass up 기회를 놓치다, 거절하다
stay up 늦게까지 자지 않다

turn up 나타나다, (TV소리) 키우다
look up (정보) 찾아보다, 방문하다, (상황) 좋아지다
come up 다가가다, 예기치 않은 일이 생기다, 다가오다
set up 준비하다, 설치하다, 일정 정하다, 누명씌우다
fill up 가득 채우다
wake up 일어나다, 깨우다
start up 시작하다, 창업하다
pick up 픽업하다, 고르다, 사다, (상황) 좋아지다
clean up 청소하다, 돈을 많이 벌다
end up 결국에는 …하게 되다
make up 화장하다, 꾸며대다, 화해하다
split up 헤어지다
take up (시간.공간) 차지하다, 취미생활을 시작하다
pull up 차를 세우다, 의자를 끌고 와 앉다
go up 올라가다, (수치) 오르다
hang up 전화를 끊다
call up 전화걸다, 컴퓨터 화면에 띄우다
blow up 파괴하다, 터트리다, 화내다
throw up 토하다, 집어치우다
back up 지원하다, (컴퓨터) 백업하다, 후진하다, 뒤로 물러서다
act up 버릇없이 굴다, 고장나다
build up 강하게 만들다, 자신감을 제고하다
cover up 은폐하다
dress up 잘 차려입다
hold up 지탱하다, 버티다, 강탈하다, 미루다
screw up 망치다
mess up 망치다, 실수하다
hit sb up 연락하다
live up 부응하다, 신나게 돈쓰며 살다
be tied up 꼼짝달싹 못하게 바쁘다
get worked up 흥분하다, 폭 빠지다
catch up with 따라잡다, 만나다, 새로운 소식 전해주다
mix up with 혼동하다
be fed up with 질리다, 싫증나다
break up with 헤어지다
hook up with 소개시켜주다, 섹스하다

set up with 소개시켜주다
keep up with 따라잡다, 연락하고 지내다, 잘 알다
come up with 좋은 생각 혹은 변명 등을 생각해내다
put up with 참다, 받아들이다
make up for 보상하다
stand up for 지지하다, 옹호하다
sign up for 들어가다, 가입하다
stick up for 편들어주다, 옹호하다
be up to …하는 중이다, 꾸미다, …을 할 수 있다
come up against 직면하다, 대항하다
calm down 진정하다, 진정되다
sit down 자리에 앉다
slow down 속도를 줄이다, 연기하다
cut down (on) 줄이다
turn down 거절하다, (소리) 줄이다, 밑으로 이동하다
go down 떨어지다, 내려가다
break down 고장나다, 신경쇠약해지다, 쉽게 설명하다
get down to 도착하다, 내려가다, 노력기울이며 시작하다
settle down 진정하다, 정착하다
fall down 넘어지다, (옷) 흘러내리다
let down 실망시키다
back down 잘못인정하다, 주장굽히다, 포기하다
close down 가게 문 닫다, 폐쇄하다
write down 기록하다, 적다
run down 뛰어내려가다, 닳아지다, 특정 정보 찾아내다, 비난하다, 고장나다
put down 기록하다, 내려놓다, 전화끊다, 진압하다, 비난하다
crack down on 진압하다, 조치를 취하다
look down on 내려다보다, 경멸하다
come down with 가벼운 병에 걸리다

Unit 03 **for·of·on**   103

look for 찾다, 구하다
wait for 기다리다

work for …에서 일하다, 효과가 있다
care for 돌보다, 좋아하다, 원하다
ask for 요청하다, 묻다, 물어보다
beg for 간청하다
leave for 출발하다, (애인과) 헤어지다
fall for 속아 넘어가다, 홀딱 반하다
stand for 상징하다, 지원하다, 편들다
search for 찾다
prepare for …할 준비를 하다
apply for 지원하다, 신청하다
apologize for 사과하다
pay for 비용을 치르다
head for 특정 방향으로 가다
start for (경기) 선수교체하다, 시작하다
file for 공식적으로 신청하다, 고소하다
root for (운동) 응원하다, 지지하다
go for 좋아하다, (가격) …로 책정되다, …하러 가다
run for 후보로 나서다, 급히 뛰어가다
vote for 찬성투표하다, 제안하다
cover for 대신 일을 처리하다, 잘못을 덮어주다
trade for 교환하다, 바꾸다
blame for 나무라다, 탓하다
take for 착각하다, 잘못알다
think of 생각하다
know of …에 대해 알고 있다
die of …로 죽다
hear of …의 소식을 듣다
take care of 돌보다, 처리하다
make fun of 비웃다
be sick of 질리다
be worthy of …할 가치가 있다
be aware of …을 알고 있다
be proud of …을 자랑스러워하다
rob ~ of 훔치다
accuse A of B 비난하다, 고소하다
inform A of B …에게 …의 정보를 주다

run short of 부족하다, 모자라다
fall short of 기대치에 이르지 못하다, 달성못하다
remind ~ of …을 보니 …가 생각나다
make a mess of 엉망으로 만들다, 망치다
put on 속이다, 무대에 올리다, 옷입다, 화장하다, 음악틀다
get on 올라타다, (기차) 타다, 잘하다
plan on 기대하다, …할 생각이다
wait on (식당) 시중들다, …을 기다리다
try on 한번 입어보다
carry on 투덜대다, 계속하다, …을 지니다
cheat on 부정행위를 하다, 몰래 바람피다
fall on 넘어지다, 책임지다, 어려움 겪다, (기념일) 언제 …이다
come on 유혹하다
count on 의지하다, 기대다
work on …의 일을 하다, 영향을 주다, 설득하다
go on 계속하다, 일어나다
insist on 주장하다, 고집하다
turn on 켜다, 성적으로 흥분되다
check on 조회하다, 확인하다
hold on 꽉잡다, 기다리다, 어려운 시기를 견디다
hit on 갑자기 생각나다, 수작걸다
grow on …가 좋아하기 시작하다
take on 책임지다, 신규채용하다, 맞서다
stand on …에 대한 특정한 입장을 갖다
be on 전원이 켜져 있다, …을 책임지다
catch on 이해가 빠르다, 유행하다
focus on 집중하다
move on 다음 일을 하다, 다른 장소로 가다, 극복하다
pick on 괴롭히다
click on 전원을 켜다, 마우스를 클릭하여 열다
pin~ on 책임을 전가하다, 고정시키다
be hard on 모질게 대하다
log on to 인터넷에 접속하다
sneak on 일러바치다, 몰래 다가가다
pass on 죽다, 건네주다, 거절하다

to·with·about

have to …해야 한다
like to …하는 것을 좋아하다
would like to 지금 …하고 싶다
come to 도착하다, 총합이 …이 되다, 의식을 되찾다
get to 일을 시작하다, 화나게 하다, 도착하다
go to (college) 학교에 진학하다
plan to …할 계획이다, …할 생각이다
try to 해보다, 시도하다
fail to 실패하다, …하지 못하다, 고장나다
happen to …에게 일어나다, 우연히 …하다
listen to 듣다, 귀를 기울이다
mean to …하려고 하다, …할 생각이다
ask~ to 요청하다, 부탁하다
take~ to …을 …로 데리고 가다
learn to …하는 것을 배우다
belong to …의 것이다
decide to …하기로 결정하다
lie to 거짓말하다
move to 이사하다, 이동하다
deserve to …할 자격이 있다
used to 과거에 …하곤 했었다
get used to …에 익숙하다, 적응하다
choose to …하기로 선택하다, 결정하다
apologize to …에게 사과하다
get back to 되돌아가다, 다시 토의하다, 다시 연락하다
afford to …할 여력이 있다
forget to …할 것을 잊다
apply to 지원하다, …와 관련이 있다, 적용되다
remember to …할 것을 기억하다
stop to …하기 위해 멈추다
agree to …에 찬성하다
commit to 전념하다, 약속하다, 충실하다
occur to 갑자기 떠오르다

owe A to B …에게 빚지다
go to work 출근하다, 일을 시작하다
come close to …에 가까이 가다, 거의 …할 뻔하다
can't stand to …을 참을 수가 없다
get ready to …할 준비가 되다
prefer A to B …보다 …을 더 좋아하다
can't wait to 몹시 …하고 싶어하다
feel free to 맘대로 …하다
have to do with …와 관련이 있다
get married to …와 결혼하다
be supposed to …하기로 되어 있다, …해야 한다
make love to 사랑을 나누다
make it to 제시간에 도착하다
reply to 응대하다, 답변하다
link to 연결하다, 링크를 걸어놓다
stick to …을 계속하다, 고수하다, 집중하다
be with …와 함께 있다, 지지하다, …의 편이다
agree with 동의하다, 찬성하다
stay with …와 함께 머물다, …의 집에 묵다, 계속하다
go with …와 함께 하다, 포함되다, 어울리다, 선택하다
meet with 만나다, 우연히 만나다
check with 물어보다, 확인하다
help ~ with 도와주다
do with …을 어떻게 하다
mess with 간섭하다, 건드리다
deal with 처리하다, 감당하다
be busy with …으로 바쁘다
be finished with …을 끝내다, 마치다
be done with …을 끝내다, 다 먹다, 헤어지다
argue with 언쟁하다, 싸우다
live with …와 함께 살다, 불쾌한 것을 참다, 견디다
think about …에 대해 생각하다
know about …에 대해 알고 있다
hear about …에 대한 소식을 듣다
forget about …을 잊다, 깜박 잊다
worrry about 걱정하다

care about 신경쓰다, 좋아하다
inquire about 문의하다
complain about 불평하다, 항의하다
bring about 야기시키다, 일으키다
come about 일어나다, 발생하다
get about 돌아다니다, 퍼지다
tweet about 트윗을 보내다

Unit 05 over·from

go over 검토하다, 조사하다, …위로 가다, 반복하다
be over 끝나다, 끝내다, 방문하다
think over 심사숙고하다
check over 철저히 조사하다, 확인하다
get over 이겨내다, 극복하다
hand over 건네주다, 책임을 전가하다
pull over 차를 길가에 대다
look over 검토하다, 살펴보다
come over 가다, 들르다, (감정) 사로잡다
stay over 머무르다, 외박하다
invite over 초대하다
tide ~ over 돕다, 당장은 …하기에 충분하다
blow over (어려움) 지나다, 폭풍이 잦아들다
fall over 바닥에 넘어지다
take over 떠맡다, 인수하다
pass over 무시하다, 대신 …을 선택하다
get off (버스, 기차) 내리다, 퇴근하다, 오르가즘에 오르다
take off 제거하다, 떠나다, 가다, 이륙하다, 쉬다, 옷벗다
drop off 차로 내려주다, 떨어트리다, 줄어들다
pay off 빚갚다, 보상받다, 성과를 내다, 뇌물주다
show off 자랑질하다, 과시하다
see off 배웅하다
put off 연기하다, 혼란하게 하다
run off with 몰래갖고 튀다, 눈맞아 도망치다

shut off 멈추게 하다, 전원끄다

piss off 열받게하다, 화나게 하다

hit it off 죽이 잘 맞다

back off 뒤로 물러서다, 진정하다

call off 취소하다

break off 관계를 끝내다, 본체로부터 떨어져나가다

kick off 행사 등을 시작하다

lay off 그만두다, 일시해고하다

rip off 훔치다, 바가지 씌우다

pull off 어려운 일을 해내다, 성공하다, 힘써서 떼어놓다

call back 다시 전화하다, 답신전화하다

bring back 돌려주다, 데려다주다, 기억나게 하다

give back 돌려주다, 환원하다

pay back 돈갚다, 복수하다

put back 다시 갖다 놓다, 연기하다

hold back 연기하다, 참다, …하는 것을 망설이다

cut back 사용을 줄이다

get ~ back 돌려받다

take ~ back 되찾다, 취소하다

come from …에서 나오다, …의 출신이다

suffer from 고생하다, 시달리다

graduate from 졸업하다

keep ~ from 비밀로 하다, …하지 못하게 하다

result from …이 원인이다

look at 쳐다보다, 살펴보다

stay at 머물다

laugh at 비웃다, 놀리다

arrive at 도착하다, 결론을 내리다

be good at …을 잘하다

jump at 덥석 물다, 포착하다

get at 영향주다, 접근하다, 도달하다, 핵심을 암시하다

come at 도달하다, 접근하다, 위협하다

work at 열심히하다

around·through 211

run away 급히 떠나다, 가출하다

walk away 그냥 가버리다

get away 도망가다, 휴가하다, 홀로 남겨두다

pass away 사망하다

stay away from 가까이하지 않다, 관여하지 않다

keep away from 가까이하지 못하게 하다

go ahead 시작하다, 선두에 서다

get ahead 앞서가다, 성공하다

come across 우연히 만나다

stop by 잠깐 들르다

come by 잠깐 들르다, 얻다

get by 최소한의 것으로 버티고 살아가다

swing by 잠깐 들르다

run ~ by 의견을 듣기 위해 …에게 설명하다

go by …에 가다, (닉네임) …으로 통하다

stand by 대기하다, 지지하다

put ~ behind 뒤에 두다, 잊다

fall behind 뒤지다, 늦어지다

leave behind …을 놔둔 채로 가다, …을 훨씬 앞서다

look forward to …을 기다리다

head towards …로 향하다

put together 함께 모으다, 준비하다, 작성하다, 정리하다

get together 만나다

put ~ through 어려움을 겪게 하다, 전화를 바꿔주다, 학비대다

be through 끝나다, 관계를 끝내다

go through 경험하다, 불쾌한 일을 견디다, 통과하다, 살펴보다

get through 이겨내다, 일을 마치다, 통화하다, 연결되다

come through 성공하다, 극복하다, 기대에 부응하다

look through 못본 척하다, 빨리 훑어보다

run through 빠르게 이동하다, 대충 읽다

do without …없이 지내다, …은 없어도 좋다

look around 둘러보다, …을 찾으러 하다

hang around 시간보내다, 어울리다

show around 구경시켜주다
fool around 시간때우다, 몰래 바람피다
get around 돌아다니다, 퍼지다, 해결하다
turn around 몸을 돌려 …하다, 상황이 호전되다
come around 의식을 되찾다, 동의하다, 들르다
stick around 머무르다
run around 돌아다니다, 바쁘다, 동시에 여러명을 사귀다, 속이다
walk around 돌아다니다
kick around 발로 걷어차다, 검토하다
be against 반대하다, …을 기대고 있다
go against 반대하다, …에게 불리해지다
look after 챙겨주다, 돌보다, 책임지고 처리하다
be after …을 찾다, 노리다
take after 닮다
inquire after 안부를 묻다
name after …의 이름을 따서 이름짓다
go along 함께 가다, 동의하다, 잘 되고 있다
come along 함께 가다, 잘 되어가다, 진행되다
get along 사이좋게 잘 지내다
tag along 함께 가다, 따라가다
fall apart 조각조각 떨어져나가다, 무너지다
tell apart 구분하다

Unit 07 **동사별 총정리**   241

Unit 01 **in·out**

in(to)
…안에, …후에, …의 상태에
ex. arrive in, go into, get into

out (of)
…안에서 밖으로, 알려져 있는, 끝까지, 완전히
ex. go out, move out,
    hear out

work in

> **영영** to be employed in a specific place
>
> **의미** …에서 일하다라고 할 때는 work for+사람 외에도 work in[at]+장소

1. Those nuns **work in** a Catholic school.
저 수녀님들은 카톨릭 학교에서 일을 하셔.

2. They think I **work at** Starbuck's. 내가 스타벅스에서 일한다고들 생각해.

A: What kind of job does your sister have? 네 누이는 어떤 직장에 다녀?

B: She **works in** a law firm downtown. 시내에 있는 법률사무소에서 일해.

turn in

> **영영** to submit something; to go to bed for the evening
>
> **의미** 1.책임자 혹은 소유자에게 제출하다 2.잠자리에 들다

1. You need to **turn in** the work by tomorrow.
넌 내일까지 일을 제출해야 돼.

2. I think that I'm going to **turn in** right now, if you don't mind.
너만 괜찮으면 지금 잠자리에 들래.

A: Make sure that you **turn in** your keys at the end of the day.
일과가 끝나면 열쇠를 제출하도록 하세요.

B: I'll leave them with the secretary. 비서한테 맡겨 놓겠습니다.

take in

영영 to ingest or put inside; to trick or fool someone; to make something smaller, especially clothing; to give shelter to someone or something

의미 1.섭취하다　2.(옷) 줄이다　3.속이다(be taken in by 사기당하다)　4.집에 머물게 하다

1. You need to **take in** healthy food. 넌 건강식을 섭취해야 돼.

2. Too many people **are taken in by** false promises.
너무 많은 사람들이 거짓 약속에 속아 넘어가.

A: So your mom lost a lot of money? 그럼 네 엄마가 많은 돈을 잃었어?

B: She **was taken in by** con men. 엄마는 사기꾼들에게 사기를 당하셨어.

drop in

영영 to visit a place or person, often unexpectedly or with short notice

의미 사전연락없이 혹은 바로 연락하고 잠깐 들르다

1. I was in the area and I thought I'd **drop in** to meet you.
이 근처에 왔다가 잠깐 들러서 볼 생각했어.

2. Visitors are welcome to **drop in** at any time.
방문객들은 언제라도 들리셔도 됩니다.

A: I heard you were at Bill and Carrie's house.
너희들 빌과 캐리 집에 있다고 들었어.

B: We decided to **drop in** and see them. 들러서 인사하려고 들르기로 했어.

Unit 01
Unit 02
Unit 03
Unit 04
Unit 05
Unit 06
Unit 07

check in

영영 to let others know you have arrived somewhere, often at places like hotels or conferences

의미 1.(호텔) 체크인하다, (공항) 탑승절차를 밟다   2.(소셜미디어) 자기가 어디에 왔다는 것을 알리다   3.확인하다

1. Is it too early to **check in**? 체크인하기엔 너무 이른가요?

2. How many pieces of luggage **are** you **checking in**?
부치실 짐이 몇 개죠?

A: When are you going to the airport? 언제 공항에 갈거야?

B: I need to **check in** for my flight by 10. 10시까지는 비행수속을 밟아야 돼.

---

check in on

영영 to find out how sb is doing; to make certain sb is safe

의미 …에게 확인하다

보충 check in on~는 …을 확인해보다, check in with sb는 …에게 왔음을 알리다, 확인하다

1. Just **check in with** Becky when you're done
네가 마치면 베키에게 확인해

2. Let's **check in on** the study group. 스터디 그룹을 확인해보자.

A: How can we get our airplane tickets? 우리는 어떻게 비행기표를 받을 수 있어?

B: We need to **check in with** the tour director.
투어책임자에게 왔다고 확인해줘야 돼.

bring in

영영 to come to a place with something; to ask an expert to come and assist

의미 1. 가지고 오다, 데려오다   2. (인재) 영입하다   3. (새로운 법 등을) 도입하다

1. Did you **bring in** the groceries? 네가 식료품들을 들여왔어?
2. We need to **bring in** someone to fix them. 바로 잡을 사람을 영입해야 돼.

A: I have decided to **bring in** an analyst to help us.
우리를 도와줄 분석가 한 사람을 영입하기로 했어.

B: Great idea! That is just what we need.
좋은 생각야! 우리가 필요한 게 바로 그거야.

believe in

영영 to trust or have faith that someone or something is good and trustworthy.

의미 …의 존재를 믿다, …가 맞다고 믿다

1. It's nice to know you **believe in** God. 신을 믿는다는 걸 아니 좋으네.
2. I need you to **believe in** us a little more! 우리를 좀 더 믿어주기를 바래!

A: Do you **believe in** ghosts? 유령이 존재한다고 생각해?
B: Yes, but I've never seen one. 어, 하지만 본 적은 없어.

engage in

- 영영 to take part or participate in something
- 의미 특정한 행위나 행동에 가담하는 것을 의미.
- 보충 약혼하다는 get[be] engaged.

1. Chris **engaged in** sex with a number of women.
   크리스는 많은 수의 여성들과 섹스를 했어.

2. She never **engages in** small talk. 걘 절대로 잡담(small talk)을 하지 않아.

A: I heard Cheryl was fired. 쉐릴이 잘렸다며.

B: She **engaged in** bad behavior. 나쁜 일에 가담했어.

major in

- 영영 to concentrate studies as a student in one specific discipline
- 의미 대학 등에서 특정과목을 전공하다
- 보충 major in 다음에 전공과목을 넣으면 된다. major는 명사로는 전공(자)라는 뜻.

1. He says he'll **major in** the study of law. 걘 법을 전공할거야.

2. Why did you **major in** European history?
   넌 왜 유럽역사를 전공한거야?

A: So you decided to **major in** science? 그래 너 과학을 전공하기로 했어?

B: Yes, I've always been interested in scientific experiments.
   응. 난 항상 과학실험에 관심을 가졌어.

hand in

영영 to submit something, especially work by students that is given to a teacher

의미 학생들이 선생님에게, 직원들이 상사에게 등 개인이 전체 책임자에게 제출하는 것.

1. It's time to **hand in** your exams. 시험지 제출해야 돼.
2. Did you **hand in** the report you were working on?
작업했던 레포트 제출했어?

A: Where are you going right now? 너 이제 어디가는거야?
B: I've got to **hand in** some library books. 도서관 책 반납해야 돼.

give in

영영 to surrender, to stop resisting; to submit to something that a person wishes to avoid

의미 1.포기하다, 굴복하다(give in to sb[sth])   2.반대하던 걸 받아들이다
3.제출하다

1. It may get tough, but I'll never **give in**. 난 절대로 포기하지 않을거야
2. Larry **gave in** when he failed the course.
래리는 그 과목에서 낙제했을 때 포기했어.

A: I am ready to quit this contest. 나 이번 대회는 그만둘 준비가 됐어.
B: Keep going. Don't **give in**! 계속 해. 포기하지마!

stay in

영영 to remain in a place, often at least overnight or for a long
period of time

의미 1. 장시간 머물다   2. 추상적으로 어떤 상태에 계속 유지하다

보충 stay in shape 몸매를 유지하다, stay in business 사업을 지속하다

1. I prefer to **stay in** a suite during business travel.
난 출장 중엔 스위트룸에 숙박하는 걸 더 좋아해.

2. I wish you could **stay in** LA a while longer. 네가 LA에 더 머무르면 좋겠어.

A: How long are you going to **stay in** Japan? 넌 일본에 얼마동안 머물거야?

B: My trip to Tokyo will last for a week. 도쿄 여행은 일주일 걸릴거야.

break in

영영 to illegally enter a building or car, especially with the
intent to steal; to give someone new experience that will
be helpful doing a job; to start to use a tool or machine
that is new

의미 1. 불법침입하다   2. 연수시키다   3. (신발, 옷) 길들이다   4. 새로운 연장이
나 도구를 쓰기 시작하다

1. Someone tried to **break in** to my apartment.
누군가가 내 아파트에 침입을 하려고 했어.

2. Robbers **broke in** to the bank. 강도들이 은행에 침입했어.

A: Why are the cops gathered outside? 왜 경찰들이 밖에 모여 있는거야?

B: Someone **broke in** the apartment beneath ours.
우리집 아래 아파트에 누군가가 침입했어.

Unit 01
Unit 02
Unit 03
Unit 04
Unit 05
Unit 06
Unit 07

fill in

> 영영 to write in missing information; to give information that a person needs; to substitute or take the place of, especially related to filling in at work
>
> 의미 1.서류의 빈 곳을 채워넣다   2.세부사항을 말해주다(fill sb in)   3.대신 일을 봐주다(fill in for sb)

1. How about you **fill in** some of the details?
너 자세한 것 좀 얘기해볼래?

2. Is there someone who can **fill in for** me? 누구 내 일 좀 봐줄 사람있어?

A: I'd like to see the doctor. 진찰 좀 받고 싶은데요.

B: Please **fill in** this form about your medical history.
이 양식에 병력(病歷)을 기입해 주세요.

enroll in

> 영영 to join a group, often in order to get an education, as in the case of a school
>
> 의미 특히 학교나 학원 등에 수강하러 등록하다, 혹은 가입하다

1. I hope to **enroll in** a course this summer.
올 여름에 한 과목 등록하고 싶어.

2. Dad decided to **enroll in** a life insurance policy.
아버지는 생명보험증서에 가입하기로 했어

A: I hope to **enroll in** a course this summer. 올 여름에 한 과목 등록하고 싶어.

B: Any course in particular? 특별히 생각하고 있는 과목이라도 있니?

keep in

> **영영** to not allow out, to restrict something
>
> **의미** 1.억제하다 2.감추다 3.나가지 못하게 하다

1. This fence is to **keep in** the cows.
   이 울타리는 소들이 나가지 못하게 하기 위한거야.

2. You'd better **keep in** the kids because it's freezing outside.
   밖이 엄청 추우니까 나가지 못하게 해.

A: Why do jails have bars on the windows?
   왜 유치장 창문에 막대기가 있는거야?

B: It helps **keep in** the prisoners. 죄수들을 가둬두는데 도움이 돼.

join in

> **영영** to enter or become a part of a group, particularly when playing team games or making music together
>
> **의미** 특히 사람들이 이미 하고 있는 일에 같이 조인하다

1. I'd like to **join in** next time you go hiking.
   네가 다음에 하이킹 갈 때 함께 하고 싶어.

2. She **joined in** when everyone began to sing.
   다들 노래부르기 시작하자 걔도 같이 불렀어.

A: Katie is very shy. 케이티는 매우 수줍어 해.

B: I'll ask her to **join in** with our games.
   난 걔보고 우리 게임하는데 같이 하자고 할거야.

step in

> **영영** to become involved, particularly in order to help in a difficult situation; to take the place of someone
>
> **의미** 논쟁이나 어려운 상황을 끝내기 위해 개입하다

1. Jack had to **step in** when his friends began arguing.
   잭은 친구들이 말싸움을 하자 참견해야 했어.

2. A new CEO will **step in** to help the failing company.
   망해가는 회사를 살리기 위해 신임 회장이 개입할거야.

A: Our manager has become very unpopular. 우리 부장 평이 아주 안좋아졌어.

B: It's about time for someone new to **step in**. 새로운 사람이 들어와야겠네.

spend~(in) ~ing

> **영영** to be somewhere for a period of time; to use money
>
> **의미** 시간을 보내다, 돈을 쓰다
>
> **보충** in은 생략되기도 한다.

1. We **spend** too much time **commuting** back and forth to work. 출퇴근에 너무 많은 시간이 걸리는 것 같아.

2. Did Jerry **spend** the day **working** here?
   제리는 여기서 하루를 일하면서 시간을 보냈어?

A: What did you do on vacation? 휴가 때 뭐했어?

B: We **spent** a few days **camping** at the beach.
   해변에서 캠핑하면서 며칠을 보냈어.

count sb in

> **영영** to express a wish to join or be a part of a group or activity
>
> **의미** …을 포함시키다 = be in

1. That sounds like a plan. **Count** me **in.** 좋은 생각이야. 나도 껴줘.
2. If you're going to the casino, **count** Dave **in.**
   너 카지노에 갈거면 데이브도 데려가.

A: Would you be interested in getting some lunch? 너 점심 좀 먹을래?

B: Sure, **count** me **in.** I'm starving. 물론. 나도 끼워줘. 배고파 죽겠어.

run in (one's family)

> **영영** to be a typical or special trait shared by family members
>
> **의미** 집안 대대로 내려오는 내력이 있다.
>
> **보충** 내력이 주어가 된다.

1. It seems to **run in your family.** 네 집안 내력인 것 같아.
2. Good looks **run in the family.** 잘 생긴 것은 집안 내력이야.

A: How did he ever get to be so ruthless?
   그 사람 어쩌면 그렇게 인정머리가 없어요?

B: I think it must **run in his family.** 집안 혈통이 그런가 봐요.

put in (time)

영영 to do something for a period of time, usually related to completing some specific work

의미 어떤 목적 달성을 하기 위해 시간이나 노력을 기울이다

보충 put in a call 전화하다, be put in jail 투옥되다, put in a good work 좋게 말해주다

1. **Put in** a few more hours and go home.
   몇시간 더 집중한 다음에 집에 가.

2. You all have clearly **put in** a lot of hard work.
   여러분들 모두 정말이지 열심히 했어요.

A: When are employees allowed to retire? 직장인들 정년퇴직이 언제야?

B: They have to **put in** at least 30 years. 적어도 30년은 일을 해야 돼.

go in for

영영 to enjoy, to seek out something because it is fun or desirable

의미 1.즐기다   2.…에 열중하다, 참가하다

1. Mary doesn't **go in for** concerts. 메리는 콘서트 가는 것을 즐기지 않아.

2. Do you **go in for** new fashions? 너 새로운 패션에 따를거야?

A: I just ate an ice cream sundae. 나 방금 아이스크림 선데를 먹었어.

B: I could **go in for** one of those. 나도 하나 먹었으면 좋겠다.

put in for

> 영영 to apply to do something, sometimes related to seeking a higher position at a job
>
> 의미 휴가나 전근 혹은 승진 등을 공식적으로 요청하다, 신청하다

1. Are you going to **put in for** a promotion?
   넌 승진신청을 정식으로 할거야?

2. The workers **put in for** a raise in pay.
   근로자들은 급여인상을 정식으로 요구했어.

A: People say you want to move away from Toronto.
   사람들이 그러는데 너 토론토에서 벗어나 다른 곳으로 이사가고 싶다며.

B: I think I'll **put in for** a transfer to another city.
   다른 도시로 전근신청을 할까봐.

fall in with

> 영영 to become a member or part of, to associate with a certain group of people
>
> 의미 1. 어울리다 2. …의 생각을 받아들이다, 수용하다

1. How did you **fall in with** your current friends?
   어떻게 지금 친구들과 어울리게 된거야?

2. I **fell in with** some people who were also traveling.
   난 여행하는 사람들과 어울리게 되었어.

A: Pete was arrested for stealing money. 피트는 돈을 훔쳐서 체포됐어.

B: He **fell in with** some bad people. 안좋은 인간들과 어울렸구나.

get involved in

> **영영** to participate, to become active in doing something; to start a new relationship with someone
>
> **의미** 1.참여하다, 연루되다   2.사람과 새로운 관계를 시작하다, 사귀다(get involved with sb)

1. Ray **was involved in** an accident. 레이가 사고를 당했어.

2. I knew I shouldn't **get involved with** him.
   난 걔와 사귀면 안된다는 것을 알고 있었어.

A: My neighbor has a lot of money. 내 이웃은 돈이 엄청 많아.

B: I think he's **involved in** banking. 은행 종사자인 것 같아.

take part in

> **영영** to participate, to actively do something = participate in
>
> **의미** 참여하다, 참가하다
>
> **보충** take part in~ 다음에는 N[~ing]이 온다.

1. I don't want to **take part in** church services.
   난 예배에 참석하고 싶지 않아.

2. I won't **take part in** the ceremony. 난 그 기념식에 참석하지 않을거야.

A: Did anyone offer you illegal drugs? 네가 불법약물을 제공한 사람이 있었어?

B: I wouldn't **take part in** something like that. 난 그런 일은 하지 않았을거야.

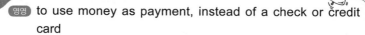

pay in cash

> **영영** to use money as payment, instead of a check or credit card
>
> **의미** 수표나 신용카드가 아니라 현금으로 계산하다
>
> **보충** 카드결제하다: pay by credit card, pay for sth with a credit card.
> 수표로 결제하다: pay by check

1. Will you **pay** for this **in cash** or by check?
   이거 현금으로 하실거예요 아니면 수표로 하실거예요?

2. I always **pay in cash** at the market. 난 시장에서 항상 현금으로 결제해.

A: You'll get a discount if you **pay in cash**.
현금으로 지불하시면 할인받으실 수 있습니다.

B: I didn't bring any cash. 현금은 하나도 안 가져 왔는 걸요.

take pride in

> **영영** to be satisfied due to taking time to do something carefully; to put special value on the work that you do
>
> **의미** 자부심을 느끼다 = be proud of = pride oneself on

1. We can **take pride in** our national team because they play nicely. 멋진 플레이를 하기 때문에 우리는 우리 국가대표팀에 자부심을 느껴.

2. Her parents must **be proud of** her. 부모님들이 자랑스러워하시겠다.

A: Your house is just beautiful! 니네 집 정말 예쁘다!

B: The carpenter **took pride in** building it. 집만든 사람이 자랑스러워 했어.

get in touch with

- **영영** to contact someone, often via the phone or e-mail
- **의미** 전화나 이멜로 연락을 취하다
- **보충** 평소에 연락을 취하고 지내는 사이라고 말하려면 get 대신에 keep, be, stay 등을 쓴다.

1. Keep trying to **get in touch with** Sam. 샘에게 연락을 계속 취해봐.
2. How can I **get in touch with** Chris?
   어떻게 크리스에게 연락을 할 수 있나요?

A: How can I **get in touch** with him? 걔에게 연락할 수 있는 방법이 없을까요?
B: You can leave me your name, and I'll tell him you called.
   성함을 말씀해주시면 전화하셨다고 전해드리겠습니다.

be into

- **영영** to be interested in or involved in something, to be actively participating in something
- **의미** 1.관심갖다, …을 하다 2.…에 열중하다, 푹 빠져 있다(be in sb)

1. My son **is into** the newest computer games.
   내 아들은 최신 컴퓨터 게임에 빠져있어.
2. I'm into gardening and landscaping.
   난 정원가꾸기와 조경에 관심이 많아.

A: You have a lot of comic books. 너 정말 만화책 많다.
B: Yeah, I'm into animation. 어, 애니메이션에 관심이 엄청 많아.

get into

영영 to become involved in, to join or start doing something

의미 1.…하기 시작하다 2.…에 빠지다 3.…에 들어가다

보충 not get into that[this] 그 얘기는 지금 하고 싶지 않다

1. Do you think I can **get into** Harvard University?
내가 하버드에 갈 수 있을 것 같아?

2. I don't want to **get into** that right now.
지금 당장 그 문제를 따지고 싶지 않아.

A: What happened between you and Carrie? 너하고 캐리 사이에 무슨 일야?
B: Well, we **got into** a fight. 어 싸웠어.

go into

영영 to enter; to give specific details about something

의미 1.…에 들어가다 2.상세히 설명하다

1. You're just asking for trouble if you **go into** his office now.
지금 그 사람 사무실에 들어가면 화를 자청하는 것밖에 안돼.

2. I need you to **go into** what happened here.
넌 여기서 무슨 일이 있었는지 자세히 말해봐.

A: Can you tell me what mistakes I made? 내가 무슨 실수를 했는지 말해줄래?
B: I don't have the time to **go into** it. 자세히 설명할 시간이 없어.

Unit 01
Unit 02
Unit 03
Unit 04
Unit 05
Unit 06
Unit 07

check into

영영 to investigate, to examine to find information; to register to stay at a hotel or similar site

의미 1.조사하다, 정보를 확인하다   2.호텔 등에 체크인하다

1. I need you to **check into** her background. 개의 배경을 조사해봐.
2. My father just **checked into** the hospital yesterday.
   아버지가 어제 병원에 입원하셨어.

A: It sounds like someone broke a window. 누가 창문을 깬 것 같아.

B: I'd better go and **check into** that. 내가 가서 확인해볼게.

run into

영영 to come upon someone or something unexpectedly; to accidentally collide with someone or something

의미 예상못한 사람이나 상황에 처하다, 부딪히다

보충 run into a little trouble 작은 곤경에 처하다, run into a traffic jam 교통체증에 걸리다

1. I hope I don't **run into** Jennifer. 난 제니퍼와 마주치지 않기를 바래.
2. If you **run into** any problems, call me. 무슨 문제 생기면 내게 전화해.

A: He's known for his smooth talking.
   그 사람은 부드러운 말 솜씨로 사람을 홀리는 것으로 유명하지.

B: I'll keep that in mind when I **run into** him next.
   다음에 마주치게 되면 그 말 명심할게.

bump into

영영 to meet unexpectedly; to mistakenly come into contact with someone or something

의미 우연히 만나다, 실수로 부딪히다, 마주치다

보충 bump into a real problem at the office today 오늘 사무실에서 진짜 어려운 문제에 직면하다

1. She **bumped into** Chris while on vacation.
   걘 휴가중에 크리스를 우연히 만났어.

2. Sorry, I didn't mean to **bump into** you. 부딪혀서 미안해요.

A: I love coming to this coffee shop. 이 커피샵에 오는게 좋아.
B: Yeah, I **bump into** my friends here. 그래, 여기서 친구들과 마주쳐.

look into

영영 to check on something or investigate; to attempt to see inside something

의미 조사하다, 자세히 안을 들여다보다

보충 look into sth, look into ~ing

1. Ted **looked into** getting a new apartment.
   테드는 새로운 아파트를 살까 진지하게 검토했어.

2. **Look into** the box and make sure you've gotten everything out of it. 그 상자안을 보고 다 비웠는지 확실히 해

A: I think Simon stole some money. 사이먼이 돈을 좀 훔친 것 같아.
B: Alright, I will **look into** the matter. 좋아, 내가 그 문제를 조사할게.

turn into

영영 to change, to become something very different; to change direction

의미 1.변화하다, …이 되다, 바뀌다   2.방향을 바꾸다

1. Jim **turns into** a fool when he's been drinking.
   짐은 술을 마시면 멍청한 짓을 해.

2. Look at you! You **turned into** such a beautiful woman!
   얘 좀 봐라! 너 아주 멋진 여자로 변했구만!

A: My sister thought she was marrying a great guy.
   내 여동생은 자기가 멋진 남자와 결혼한다고 생각했어.

B: But he **turned into** a lazy, boring husband.
   하지만 그 남자는 게으르고 지겨운 남편이 되었지.

fall into

영영 to accidentally go into something; to begin something without having planned to do it

의미 1.…한 상태가 되다   2.계획에 없던 일을 시작하게 되다

1. Helen **fell into** her writing career while at university.
   헬렌은 대학에서 작가로서의 경력을 시작했어.

2. The injury occurred when he **fell into** a ditch.
   그 상처는 걔가 도랑에 빠졌을 때 생겼어.

A: Why are all of these barriers here? 이 모든 장애물들이 여기에 있는거야?

B: They prevent people from **falling into** the construction site.
   사람들이 건설현장에 빠지지 않도록 하는거야.

tap into

영영 to connect with something, specifically to use it for personal benefit; to extract something from a source

의미 1.두드리다 2.접근하다, 활용하다 3. ···자료를 얻다

보충 tap in= 폰이나 컴퓨터 키를 눌러 정보나 숫자를 입력하는 것.

1. The candidate tapped into some wealthy supporters.
그 후보는 일부 돈많은 지원자들에게 접근했어.

2. I plan to tap into a new source of income.
난 새로운 소득원을 이용할 계획이야.

A: How did they know all of that personal information?
걔네들이 어떻게 그 모든 개인정보를 얻었대?

B: Someone tapped into our e-mails. 누군가 우리 이멜을 뒤져봤어.

sneak into

영영 to get into an area in an improper or illegal way

의미 몰래 들어가다

1. Some kids sneak into kitchens to get candy.
캔디를 갖기 위해 부엌에 몰래 들어가는 아이들이 있어.

2. I had to sneak into my girlfriend's apartment.
난 여친 아파트에 몰래 들어가야 했어.

A: We aren't allowed to go inside. 우리는 안으로 들어가면 안돼.

B: Let's sneak into the back entrance. 뒷문으로 몰래 들어가자.

break into

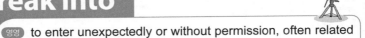

영영 to enter unexpectedly or without permission, often related to entering a building illegally to steal items

의미 1. 뭔가 훔치기 위해 침입하다 2. …하기 시작하다, 갑자기 …을 터트리다
3. 새로운 분야에 뛰어들다

1. **The thieves break into the vacant house.** 도둑들이 빈집에 침입했어.

2. **Sounds like it would be a tough area to break into.**
새롭게 시장을 공략하기는 어렵겠구나.

A: **This safe is where I store all of my money.**
내돈 전부를 보관하고 있는 금고야.

B: **No one could break into a safe like that.**
그런 금고라면 아무도 깨부수지 못할거야.

---

talk ~into

영영 to persuade, to convince someone to do something

의미 설득해서 …하게 하다

보충 ↔ talk sb out of~

1. **You talked me into it.** 네가 그거 하라고 했잖아.

2. **I talked him into staying here.** 난 걔를 설득해서 여기에 남도록 했어.

A: **Is Rob lending us his car?** 랍이 우리한테 차를 빌려줄까?

B: **I can talk him into it.** 내가 설득해서 그렇게 하도록 할 수 있어.

Unit 01
Unit 02
Unit 03
Unit 04
Unit 05
Unit 06
Unit 07

look out

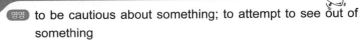

> **영영** to be cautious about something; to attempt to see out of something
>
> **의미** 조심하다
>
> **보충** look out for sb 돌보다(take care of), 조심하다

1. I **look out** the window and saw the mailman. 창문밖으로 우체부를 봤어.
2. **Look out for** people who are trying to cheat you.
   네게 사기치려고 하는 사람들을 조심해.

A: I'm going to go to a nightclub. 나 나이트클럽에 갈거야.

B: **Look out for** men who just want to sleep with you. 너와 자려하는 남자들 조심해.

hang out

> **영영** to remain somewhere casually, without doing a specific task; to protrude or stick out; to put articles of clothing outside, usually to dry
>
> **의미** 1.시간을 보내다, 어울리다 2.몸을 내밀다 3.말리기 위해 옷 등을 밖에 내놓다
>
> **보충** hang out with sb ⋯와 어울리다 = hang around with sb

1. It is a good place for couples or friends to **hang out.**
   커플이나 친구들이 어울려 놀기에 좋은 장소야.
2. Why don't you stay here and just **hang out with** us?
   여기 남아서 우리와 놀자.

A: It takes 2 hours for me to get home. I should get going.
   집에 가는데 두 시간 걸려. 가야 돼.

B: Stay a little longer to **hang out with** me. 더 남아서 나랑 놀자.

find out

> **영영** to learn information that was unknown before, to learn the answer to a question
>
> **의미** 사실이나 정보 등을 알아내다. find out (about) sth, find out (wh~)
>
> **보충** find는 물리적으로 찾다, 발견하다

1. When you **find out** the results, please give me a call.
   결과 알게 되면 전화해주라.

2. How did you **find out** she slept with Chris?
   걔가 크리스하고 잤다는 걸 어떻게 알아냈어?

A: I'll leave before this movie ends.   이 영화가 끝나기 전에 난 갈거야.

B: Don't you want to find out what happened?   어떻게 되는지 알고 싶지 않아?

check out

> **영영** to look carefully at something; to investigate for possible problems; to pay for items at a store
>
> **의미** 1.꼼꼼히 확인하다 2.퇴실절차밟다 3.계산대에서 계산하다 4.(도서관) 책을 빌리다
>
> **보충** Check it out! 이것 봐봐!

1. Guests need to **check out** by 11:00 am.
   투숙객은 오전 11시까지 체크아웃해야 됩니다.

2. Hey, **check out** that girl! She is really hot!   저 여자봐봐! 정말 섹시하다!

A: We have got to check out those new cell phones.
   우리 저 새로 나온 핸드폰을 확인해봐야겠어.

B: Let's do it right now.   지금 확인해보자.

give out

> **영영** to fail or no longer work properly; to distribute something to others
>
> **의미** 1.바닥이 나다, 정지하다 2.배포하다, 나누어주다 3.(빛) 발하다
>
> **보충** 바닥이 나다, 작동이 멈춘다는 Sth gives out~의 형태로.

1. I've never known the teacher to **give out** homework.
선생님이 숙제를 나눠주는 걸 본 적이 없어.

2. Are you going to **give out** the pamphlets? 넌 팜플렛을 나눠줄거야?

A: How did you get the concert tickets? 콘서트 티켓을 어떻게 구했어?

B: My boss **gave** them **out** to us. 사장이 우리에게 나눠줬어.

move out

> **영영** to leave a place of residence; to leave together as a military or police force
>
> **의미** 1.이사나가다 2.(경찰 등이) 출동하다
>
> **보충** move in 이사오다, move in with 동거하다, move to …로 이사가다, move from …로부터 이사오다, move away 이사가버리다

1. I may have to **move out** to Paris for my job.
일 때문에 파리로 이사가야 할지도 몰라.

2. The soldiers **moved out** toward the next town.
군인들이 다음 마을로 이동했다.

A: Why aren't you staying at the guest house?
왜 게스트 하우스에 머물지 않는거야?

B: I thought it'd be better if I **moved out**. 내가 나가면 더 좋을거라 생각했어.

leave out

영영 to exclude or not allow; to keep something outside

의미 1.제외하다, 빼놓다   2.밖에 두다

보충 feel left out 소외감을 느끼다

1. The report **left out** some important stuff.
   그 보고서는 몇몇 중요한 사항들을 빠트렸어

2. Just **leave out** the boring details. 지루한 세부적인 것들은 제외시켜.

A: Do you think Karen was being honest? 카렌이 솔직했다고 생각해?

B: No, she **left out** some things intentionally.
   아니, 걘 일부러 몇가지 사실들을 누락했어.

break out

영영 to escape a place where a person is not allowed to leave;
to develop very quickly and unexpectedly into something
special; to spread a contagious disease or illness

의미 1.도망가다, 탈주하다   2.(발진, 종기 등이) 나다   3.별안간 …하기 시작하
다   4.(전쟁, 전염병) 발발하다

1. They say several prisoners **broke out** tonight.
   오늘밤 몇몇 죄수들이 탈옥했어.

2. The fire **broke out** last night. 화재가 어젯밤에 발생했어.

A: A serious flu epidemic **broke out** this week.
   이번주에 심각한 전염성 독감이 발생했어.

B: That may result in some people dying. 사람들이 일부 죽게 될지도 몰라.

Unit 01
Unit 02
Unit 03
Unit 04
Unit 05
Unit 06
Unit 07

pick out

영영 to choose something that a person prefers; to remove something from a group of similar items

의미 선택하다, 고르다, 제외시키다

보충 pick out for~ …로 선택하다. pick out of~ …중에서 선택하다

1. I'm going to help you **pick out** dresses this afternoon.
내가 오늘 오후에 드레스 고르는 것 도와줄 게.

2. **Pick out** some that you like. 맘에 드는거 좀 골라.

A: How did you **pick out** your car? 네 차는 어떻게 고른거야?

B: It was the most expensive car available. 구할 수 있는 가장 비싼 차였어.

see out

영영 to go with someone to the door as they are leaving, usually as a way of being polite

의미 문 밖까지 나와서 잘가라고 인사하다, 배웅하다

보충 *cf.* see off 배웅하다

1. Excuse me, I must **see out** some guests. 잠깐만, 나 손님들 배웅해야 돼.

2. She was too busy to **see** me **out** after our visit.
갠 너무 바빠 우리가 방문하고 가는데 배웅을 못했어.

A: Let me **see** you **out**. 문까지 배웅할게.

B: Don't worry. I can **see** myself **out**. 내가 알아서 나갈게.

help out

영영 to give assistance or aid to someone who needs it; to assist someone to leave

의미 1.곤경에 처한 사람을 도와주다　2.나오도록 도와주다

보충 help sb out with~ …가 …하는 것을 도와주다

1. I was just doing my job. I was glad to **help out**.
   제 일을 한 것 뿐인데요. 도와주게 되어 기뻤어요.

2. Are you going to **help** me **out** with this or not?
   이것 좀 도와줄거야 말거야?

A: Do you teach for a living? 가르치는 게 직업인가요?

B: No, I only volunteer to **help out** others.
   아니요. 자원봉사로 다른 사람들을 돕는 것뿐이예요.

hand out

영영 to distribute items to others, often when a teacher distributes paperwork to students

의미 1.선생님이 학생에게 시험지를 나눠주듯 나눠주다　2.뭔가 정보를 건네다

보충 hand out sth to sb …에게 …을 나눠주다, handout n. 유인물

1. I have to get the teacher to **hand out** the tests.
   그 선생님이 내게 시험지들을 나눠주도록 했어.

2. I want you to have a **handout** ready to distribute at the meeting Monday. 월요일 회의에서 나누어 줄 유인물을 준비해 두길 바래

A: Could you **hand out** these exams? 이 시험지 나눠줄래?

B: Sure, I'll give one to each student. 예. 각 학생에게 한부씩 줄게요.

stand out

> **영영** to be shown to be special or different from most others
> **의미** 눈에 잘 띄다, 두드러지다
> **보충** stand out in a crowd 사람들 속에서 두드러지다

1. He **stands out** in a crowd because he's so tall.
갠 키가 커서 군중 속에서 두드러져 보여.

2. This is the kind of guy who wants to **stand out** in a crowd.
군중 속에서 돋보이고 싶어하는 그런 종류의 놈이야.

A: Why are you always writing reports? 왜 늘상 보고서를 쓰는거야?
B: I'm going to try to **stand out** at work. 직장에서 두드러져 보일려고.

fill out

> **영영** to write down information related to questions, particularly on an application; to gain weight or get heavier
> **의미** 1.서류의 빈칸을 채워넣다, 작성하다 2.살이 찌다
> **보충** fill in the blanks 서류의 빈 곳에 채워넣다, 기입하다, 알아맞추다

1. Just **fill out** this form and I'll bring you a receipt.
이 양식을 작성하시면 제가 영수증을 가져다 드리죠.

2. Your son **has filled out** since he turned 10 years old.
네 아들은 열살 때부터 살이 찌기 시작했어.

A: Don't forget to **fill out** those forms before you go.
가기 전에 이 양식을 다 채우는 것 잊지마.
B: I'll leave them on your desk before I go. 제가 가기 전에 책상 위에 둘게요.

point out

영영 to focus attention on something specific, to show something to be important

의미 지적하다, 언급하다, 가리키다

보충 point out sth, point out to sb, point out that S+V

1. I'll **point out** the new president to you. 네게 새로운 사장을 가르쳐줄게.

2. Did I **point out** how this will benefit you?
이게 네게 어떻게 이로울거라고 내가 언급했어?

A: What did Jim say to you? 짐이 네게 뭐라고 했어?

B: He wanted to **point out** some important details.
좀 중요한 세부사항을 언급하고 싶었었대.

work out

영영 to conclude successfully; to exercise for better physical health; to clarify the details of something

의미 1.잘되다, 잘 풀리다 2.운동하다 3.해결하다

보충 work out 근육훈련 등 체육관에서 운동하다. exercise는 다양한 방식으로 운동하다

1. You need to **work out** to stay in shape. 몸매유지하려면 운동을 해야 돼.

2. I was engaged last year, but it didn't **work out.**
작년에 약혼했는데 잘 안 되었어.

A: I'm nervous because I owe so much money. 빚이 너무 많아 짜증나.

B: Things will **work out** all right. Just relax. 다 잘 될 거야. 진정하라고.

figure out

영영 to learn the meaning of something or the solution to a problem

의미 이해하다, 해결책을 알아내다

보충 figure out+의문사~ 의 형태가 많이 쓰인다. That[It] figures는 "내 그럴 줄 알았어"

1. Tim and I didn't get it at first either, but then we **figured** it **out.** 팀과 나 모두 처음에 이해못했지만 나중에 이해하게 되었어.

2. I'd like you to help me **figure out** what's wrong with this printer. 이 프린터 뭐가 문제인지 알아내는 데 좀 도와줘.

A: Did you solve the puzzle? 그 퍼즐 풀었어?

B: No, I didn't **figure** it **out.** 아니, 난 못 알아냈어.

watch out

영영 to pay attention for something; to be cautious or careful about something or to avoid something

의미 주의하다, 조심하다

보충 watch out for sb[sth] …을 조심하다, …에게 나쁜 일이 생기지 않도록 하다

1. **Watch out for** people who are dishonest. 정직하지 못한 사람들을 조심해.

2. **Watch out!** You almost hit the car! 조심해! 차 칠뻔했잖아!

A: I'm going to take a taxi. 나 택시탈거야.

B: **Watch out for** dishonest taxi drivers. 속여먹는 기사들 조심해.

ask out

영영 to invite someone somewhere, often on a date

의미 데이트 신청하다

보충 ask out on a date 데이트 신청하다

1. I'm thinking about **asking** her **out** on a date.
   난 걔한테 데이트 신청을 해볼까 생각중이야.

2. I actually came here to **ask** you **out**. 실은 데이트 신청하러 왔어.

A: I want to **ask** Jill **out** on a date. 질에게 데이트 신청하고 싶어.

B: You got the wrong idea. She already has a boyfriend.
   잘못 짚었어. 걘 이미 남친이 있어.

make out

영영 to kiss and have physical interactions with a romantic partner, and possibly sex

의미 1.이해하다   2.알아보다   3.성공하다   4.섹스를 포함한 애정행위(~with sb)

보충 How is sb making out~ ? …가 (…에서) 잘 지내고 있어?

1. How **is** Terry **making out** in her new job?
   테리는 새로운 직장에서 어떻게 지내?

2. Her parents caught her **making out with** her boyfriend.
   걔는 부모에게 남친과 애무하는 장면을 들켰어.

A: How did you **make out** at the lawyer's office?
   그 변호사 사무실에서 어떤 식으로 일이 됐어?

B: In the end everything worked out for the best.
   결국에는 모든 일이 가장 좋게 해결됐어.

hold out

영영 to refuse to do something, even though others may choose to do it

의미 1.굴복하지 않다, 어려운 상황에서 지속하다, 계속하다   2.희망하다, 기대하다

보충 not hold hope~ …라는 희망을 갖지 않다, hold out for 요구하다

1. Sam **is holding out** until things get better.
   샘은 상황이 좋아질거라고 기대하고 있어.

2. You should **hold out for** something bigger. 뭔가 더 큰 것을 요구해.

A: I miss my ex-girlfriend so much. 난 전 여친이 정말 많이 보고 싶어.

B: You can't **hold out** hope she will come back. 걔가 돌아올거라는 희망갖지마.

---

burn out

영영 to work too hard and lose enthusiasm or interest for the work; to be consumed with flames until nothing is left to burn

의미 1.완전히(out) 타다(burn), 다 타다   2.완전히 지치다

보충 burnout 극도의 피로감

1. Working twenty hours a day left Lisa **burned out.**
   하루에 20시간 일해서 리사는 완전 골아떨어졌어.

2. There is a lot of **burnout** among lawyers.
   변호사들 사람들에게서는 극도의 피로감이 있어.

A: You had a great job. Why did you quit? 넌 일을 아주 잘했는데, 왜 그만뒀어?

B: I felt I was starting to **burn out.** 골아떨어지기 시작하고 있다는 느낌이 들었어.

set out

> **영영** to start to do something with a very specific goal; to begin a journey; to place something outside
>
> **의미** 1.(여행 등) 시작하다, 목표를 갖고 뭔가 시작하다   2.물건을 밖에 두다
>
> **보충** set out for~ …로 출발하다, set out on~ …을 시작하다, set out to+V …하기 시작하다

1. We'll **set out for** New York on Friday.
   우리는 금요일에 뉴욕을 향해 출발할거야.

2. She **set out for** her mother's house.   걘 자기 엄마 집으로 갔어.

A: I **set out to** become a successful businessman.
   성공한 비즈니스맨이 되기 위해 뛰기 시작했어.

B: Well, I would say you've achieved your goal.   넌 네 목표를 달성할거야.

take out

> **영영** to accompany someone, often a female on a date; to remove from a place
>
> **의미** 1.잡아서 밖으로(out) 꺼내다   2.데리고 나가다   3.제거하다
>
> **보충** takeout 포장음식물

1. Could you **take out** the garbage bag?   쓰레기봉투 좀 내갈테야?

2. Lisa got **takeout** from the Chinese restaurant.
   리사는 중국식당에서 음식을 포장해왔어.

A: Is there anything else that I have to do before I can go home?
   집에 가기전에 해야할 일이 더 있습니까?

B: Yes. Sweep the floor and **take out** the trash.
   바닥을 닦고 쓰레기를 치우라고.

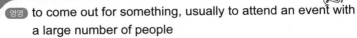

turn out

영영 to come out for something, usually to attend an event with a large number of people

의미 1모습을 드러내다   2(일이 …하게) 진행되다   3드러나다, 밝혀지다

보충 turn sth out 전열기구 등을 끄다

1. Don't worry. Things always **turn out** for the best.
걱정마 다 잘될거야.

2. Let's make it a rule to **turn out** the lights every night.
밤에는 언제나 전등을 끄기로 합시다.

A: Why did you break up with Chris? 너 왜 크리스하고 헤어졌어?

B: He **turned out** to be just another two-timer. 걘 바람둥이에 지나지 않았어.

pass out

영영 to faint, to lose consciousness, often due to illness or drunkenness

의미 병이나 음주로 인해 졸도하다, 의식을 잃다

1. The hot weather caused her to **pass out.**
날씨가 너무 더워서 걔는 정신을 잃었어.

2. I **passed out** when I hit my head. 내가 머리를 부딪혔을 때 졸도했어.

A: What happened when you told her the bad news?
네가 걔에게 안좋은 소식을 말했을 때 어땠어?

B: She was shocked and she **passed out.** 충격을 받고 의식을 잃었어.

black out

영영 to be unable to remember a period of time, often caused by drunkenness or some unusual event

의미 1.정신을 잃다, 의식을 잃다   2.정전되다

1. The crash happened after the driver **blacked out.**
운전자가 의식을 잃은 후에 충돌사고가 발생했어.

2. If you drink whiskey, you'll **black out.**
위스키를 마시면, 정신을 잃게 될거야.

A: I **blacked out** during my birthday celebration.
생일파티하다 의식을 잃었어.

B: Well, everyone kept buying you drinks. 저기, 다들 계속 네게 술을 사줬지.

stress out

영영 to do something to cause someone to become anxious, nervous or upset

의미 타인에게 스트레스를 주다

보충 be stressed out 스트레스를 받아 지치다

1. You **look stressed out.** What's wrong?
스트레스에 지쳐 빠진 것 같으네. 무슨 일이야?

2. We **were stressed out** by the schedule.
우리는 일정 때문에 완전히 뻗었어.

A: Sorry, I didn't mean that. 미안, 그럴 의도는 아니었어.

B: I guess you're a little **stressed out** right now.
지금 너 스트레스 좀 받은 것 같아.

win out

영영 to become the eventual winner or champion in a competition; to be selected over others

의미 1.(어려움을 이기고) 이기다, 승리하다 2.선택되다

1. Eventually, one of the contestants will **win out.**
결국, 경쟁자 중 한 명이 이기게 될거야.

2. The best team **won out** during the tournament.
최고의 팀이 토너먼트 경기에서 이겼어.

A: This is a competition for the best cake recipe.
이건 최고의 케익레시피 경연대회야.

B: Which of these cakes is going to **win out?** 이 케익 중 어떤게 이길 것 같아?

eat out

영영 to have a meal at a restaurant instead of at home

의미 식당에서 외식하다

1. We've been **eating out** a lot lately. 우린 최근에 외식을 아주 많이 했어.

2. I have to **eat out** when I'm traveling. 난 여행중에 외식을 해야 돼.

A: How do you want to spend the day? 하루를 어떻게 보내고 싶어?

B: Let's catch a movie and **eat out** tonight. 영화보고 저녁에 외식하자.

blow out

영영 to use air to stop a flame; to experience a punctured tire while driving; in slang, to have a big or special event that is very extravagant

의미 1.불을 불어 끄다   2.쉽게 이기다   3.운전 중 자동차가 펑크나다   4.큰 파티를 열다

보충 blowout 낙승, 펑크, 잔치

1. The tire **blow out** stopped our trip to the mountains.
   타이어가 펑크나서 산으로 가다가 멈췄어.

2. You can **blow out** the candles when we're finished.
   우리가 끝나면 불어서 촛불을 꺼.

A: You took a long time to get home.   집에 오는데 시간이 오래걸렸다.

B: My tire **blew out,** and I needed to change it.   타이어가 펑크나서 갈아야 했어.

sell out

영영 to have people purchase all of the merchandise for sale; (this is slang) to give up personal principles in order to gain financial profit

의미 1.다 팔다, 다 팔리다   2.이익을 위해 신념을 버리다

보충 sell sb out 배신하다

1. Hopefully the tickets will **sell out.**   다행스럽게도, 표는 다 팔릴거야.

2. The artist **sold out** when he began working for businesses.
   그 예술가는 사업을 시작했을 때 신념을 버렸어.

A: I thought you were going to buy a heater.   너 히터 살거라 생각했는데.

B: They **were sold out** by the time I got there.   내가 갔을 때 다 팔렸어.

chew out

> **영영** to yell at or berate someone for something they did wrong
> **의미** 호되게 꾸짖다, 야단치다

1. The boss will **chew** you **out** if you're late.
   네가 지각하면 사장이 호되게 꾸짖을거야.

2. He **was chewed out** by the army sergeant.
   걔는 육군하사로부터 혼났어.

A: Why are you sneaking into your house? 왜 네 집에 몰래 들어가는거야?

B: I don't want to **get chewed out** by my dad for being late.
   늦었다고 아버지한테 혼나기 싫어서.

keep out

> **영영** to not allow inside, to forbid from entering
> **의미** 들여보내지 않다, 출입을 금지하다
> **보충** Keep out of this! 끼어들지마!. Keep out of my way! 비키세요!

1. The guards **keep out** people who aren't allowed.
   경비들이 출입허가되지 않은 사람들을 들여보내지 않고 있어.

2. Just **keep out** of this argument. 이 논쟁에 끼어들지마.

A: You couldn't enter the government building?
   너 정부건물에 들어갈 수가 없었어?

B: We were told to **keep out** or we'd be arrested.
   출입을 금한다고 들었고 아니면 체포될거였어.

hear sb out

> 영영 to take the time to listen to what someone wants to say
> 의미 중간에 말을 끊지 않고 끝까지 듣다

1. Please, **hear** me **out**. This is important. 좀 잘 들어봐. 중요하다고.
2. I'm glad you decided to **hear** me **out**.
   내 말을 끝까지 들어주기로 해서 고마워.

A: **Hear** me **out**, and I think you'll agree with me.
   내 말 좀 끝까지 들어봐. 그럼 내 말에 동의할거야.
B: No, I really am not interested in your opinion.
   아니, 난 정말이지 네 의견에 관심없어.

freak out

> 영영 to act wild, angry or upset for a short time due to something strange or unusual happening
> 의미 이상한 일 때문에 깜짝 놀라다, 어찌할 바를 모르다, 화가 나다
> 보충 freak sb out …을 놀라게 하다, a speed freak 스피드광

1. I feel really bad about how I **freaked** you **out**.
   널 놀래켜서 정말 미안해.
2. I **got so freaked out** that I hung up the phone.
   너무 놀라 전화를 끊었어.

A: Was your mom scared when she saw the mouse?
   네 엄마는 쥐를 봤을 때 놀래셨어?
B: Oh yeah, she completely **freaked out**. 그럼, 완전히 질겁하셨어.

get out

- **영영** to leave an area, often in a fast or unexpected manner
- **의미** 나가다
- **보충** **get sb out** 내보내다. **get out of~** …을 하지 않다. **get out of+장소** …에서 나오다. **Get out of here!** 꺼져!, 그럴리가!

1. Run for your life! **Get out of** the building! 도망쳐! 빌딩에서 나가!

2. I just **got out of** the hospital. 나 방금 병원에서 퇴원했어

A: How can I **get out of** going to that party?
어떻게 하면 그 모임에 빠질 수 있을까?

B: Tell them that you're not feeling well. 몸이 안좋다고 말해버려.

go out

- **영영** to travel in order to do something specific
- **의미** 1. …을 하기 위해 밖으로 나가다, 외출하다 2. (전기, 불) 꺼지다
- **보충** **go out ~ing, go out to+V** …하러 나가다. **go out with sb** 함께 나가다, 데이트하다

1. It's too cold. Don't **go out.** You might catch a cold.
너무 추워. 나가지 마. 감기걸릴지 몰라.

2. Let's **go out.** I'll show you around the city.
나가자. 이 도시를 구경시켜줄게.

A: Where did the girls go? 여자애들 어디갔어?

B: They **went out** to do some shopping. 쇼핑 좀 하러 나갔어.

drop out

> **영영** to quit or stop doing something, often related to quitting school
>
> **의미** 학교나 경기 등을 중간에 그만두다
>
> **보충** drop out of school 중퇴하다, dropout 중퇴자

1. I never planned to **drop out** of the club.
난 전혀 그 클럽에서 중도하차 할 생각이 없었어.

2. Please don't **drop out** of the program. 프로그램을 중간에 그만두지마.

A: My brother dropped out of school at 19. 내 형은 19세에 중퇴했어.

B: Why did he **drop out** of university? 왜 대학을 중퇴했어?

come out

> **영영** to venture out of a building or area; to publicly announce you are gay
>
> **의미** 1.…에서 나오다   2.게이임을 밝히다

1. I can **come out** in a few minutes. 난 몇분 후에 나올 수 있어.

2. Terry **came out** to his parents yesterday.
테리는 어제 부모에게 게이라고 밝혔어.

A: Tell the people in the lobby to **come out**.
로비에 있는 사람들에게 나오라고 해.

B: They are waiting for their friends to arrive.
걔네들 친구들이 도착하기를 기다리고 있어.

stay out of

> **영영** to avoid going somewhere; to avoid becoming involved with something
>
> **의미** …로부터 벗어나 있다라는 말로 안 좋은 일에 개입하거나 끼지 말다
>
> **보충** Stay out of this! 관여하지마!. Stay out of trouble! 말썽피지마!

1. If you don't know enough about something, **stay out of** it.
   뭘 모르면 끼어들지마.

2. He told us to **stay out of** his driveway. 자기 주차장에 얼씬하지 말라고 했어.

A: The Johnsons are having marital problems. 존슨 씨네는 부부문제가 있어.

B: Just **stay out of** their personal lives. 개인사에는 관여하지마.

grow out of

> **영영** to get older and no longer be interested in something or engage in some habit; to grow taller and no longer be able to fit into certain clothing; to originate from
>
> **의미** 1. 나이 들어 습관 등을 그만두다 2. …에서 생기다 3. 커서 예전 옷을 못 입다

1. Kevin **grew out of** his clothes when he was a teenager.
   케빈은 십대가 된 후에 옷이 작아 못입었어.

2. Their anger **grew out of** an argument.
   걔네들의 분노는 한 논쟁 중에 생겼어.

A: Carla and Brian were friends before they began dating.
   칼라와 브라이언은 데이트하기 전에는 친구였어.

B: Their love **grew out of** their friendship. 우정이 애정으로 싹튼거지.

sneak out

영영 to leave quietly or secretly, in a way that no one knows the person is gone

의미 들키지 않고 몰래 빠져나가다

보충 ↔ sneak into 몰래 들어오다

1. Are you too busy to **sneak out** with me for a walk?
   너무 바빠서 나랑 잠깐 나가 산책못한다고?

2. We **snuck out** before the performance ended.
   우리는 공연이 끝나기 전에 빠져나왔어.

A: Are there any teachers in the hall? 복도에 선생님 계셔?

B: The coast is clear. You can **sneak out** of school now.
   안전해. 이제 학교에서 빠져나와도 돼.

talk sb out of

영영 to persuade someone not to do something

의미 설득하여 …하지 못하게 하다(talk sb out of+명사[~ing])

1. You won't be able to **talk** her **out of** punishing you.
   넌 걔를 설득해서 널 혼내지 말아달라고 할 수 없을거야.

2. You want me to **talk** you **out of** it?
   내가 널 설득해서 그걸 못하게 해달라고?

A: It's stupid for Cindy to get married; she's just too young.
   신디가 결혼하는건 어리석은 짓이야. 너무 어려.

B: I know, but I couldn't **talk** her **out of** it. 알아. 하지만 설득을 할 수가 없었어.

miss out on

> **영영** to have lost the chance to do something that would have been fun or beneficial
>
> **의미** 좋은 기회를 놓치다
>
> **보충** miss out on+sth[~ing], miss out on a chance to+V …할 기회를 놓치다

1. I don't want to **miss out on** the holidays with my kids.
애들과 함께하는 명절을 놓치고 싶진 않아.

2. He **missed out on** a chance to make a lot of money.
걔는 많은 돈을 벌 기회를 놓쳤어.

A: I can't go to the celebration tonight. 오늘밤 기념축하연에 못가.

B: Don't **miss out on** the chance to have some fun!
재미있게 놀 수 있는 기회를 놓치지마!

up·down

up
위로, 오르는, 접근, 완전히, 다
ex. go up, get up, set up

down
아래로, 낮은, 완전히, 꽉, 줄어든
ex. sit down, shut down,
     cut down

get up

영영 to stand, to rise from a seated position

의미 1.잠에서 깨어 일어나다   2.자리에서 일어나다

보충 get sb up …을 깨우다, get up late 늦잠자다

1. I have to **get up** early and catch that plane for New York.
일찍 일어나서 뉴욕행 비행기를 타야 돼.

2. I'm sorry to **get** you **up** so early.   너무 일찍 깨워서 미안해.

A: Do you need to **get up** early tomorrow morning?
내일 아침 일찍 일어나야 돼?

B: Yeah. Please set the alarm at 5 a.m.   어. 5시로 알람 좀 해줘.

show up

영영 to arrive for an appointment or gathering; to embarrass someone by exposing faults or problems

의미 1.회의나 약속 장소에 나타나다. 모임에 나오다, 도착하다   2.(곤란한 문제로) 당황하게 하다

보충 show up at the seminar 세미나에 참석하다, 참석예정인 사람이 안나오는 경우는 a no-show

1. How come she didn't **show up** at the meeting this morning?
어째서 걔는 오늘 아침 회의에 나오지 않은거야?

2. Sara was **a no-show** at our wedding.   새라는 우리 결혼식에 오지 않았어.

A: What time is the driver supposed to **show up**?
기사가 언제 오기로 되어 있어?

B: He should be here any minute now.   올 때가 다 됐어.

cheer up

영영 to make someone feel better, especially if the person is sad or depressed

의미 기운내다, 기운나게 하다(cheer sb up)

보충 Cheer up!(기운내!)

1. You'll have a good job interview. **Cheer up.** 면접을 잘 볼거야. 기운내.

2. There's nothing like a night out to **cheer** you **up.**
   저녁에 외출하는 것만큼 기운나는건 없어.

A: Why do you look so unhappy? **Cheer up.** 왜 그리 안 좋아 보여? 힘내.

B: I'm really worried because my mom is in the hospital.
   어머니가 병원에 계셔서 정말 걱정돼.

give up

영영 to quit or surrender; to stop an effort to do something

의미 뭔가 하다가 그만두다, 포기하다(give up sth[~ing])

보충 give up on sb …을 포기하다, 단념하다

1. I don't want you to **give up** your career.
   난 네가 커리어를 포기하지 않기를 원해.

2. Tony **gave up** smoking at last. 토니는 마침내 담배피는걸 포기했어.

A: Maybe I shouldn't study acting. 난 연기공부를 하지 말아야 될 것 같아.

B: Come on, don't **give up** your dreams. 그러지마, 네 꿈을 포기하지마.

hurry up

> **영영** to move more quickly, to speed up
>
> **의미** 행동을 서둘러 하다, 서두르다
>
> **보충** 서둘러 …하다 hurry up and+V, hurry up with sth

1. **Hurry up** and make up your mind. 어서 빨리 마음을 결정해.

2. You'd better **hurry up.** We might be late. 서둘러. 늦을지 몰라

A: **Hurry up,** we're going to be late. 서둘러. 우리 늦겠어.

B: I just need time to put on my make-up. 화장 좀 할 시간이 필요해.

bring up

> **영영** to introduce a new subject; to raise a child; to vomit or upheave
>
> **의미** 1.아이를 양육하다(raise) 2.대화의 화제를 꺼내다 3.컴퓨터 스크린에 …을 띄우다 4.토하다
>
> **보충** I don't want to bring this up, 이 얘기를 꺼내기 싫지만

1. This time don't **bring up** what happened at the last meeting.
이번에는 지난 번 회의 때 나왔던 이야기는 하지 맙시다.

2. Can you **bring up** the list of candidates again?
다시 한번 후보자 리스트를 화면에 띄워볼래?

A: I want to talk about a few things. 몇가지 얘기하고 싶어.

B: Please don't **bring up** anything upsetting. 속상한 얘기는 꺼내지마.

grow up

영영 to mature, to become an adult

의미 성장하다, 자라다

보충 grow up to be sb 커서 …가 되다

1. I'm going to be a star when I **grow up!** 난 커서 스타가 될거야!

2. He **grew up to be** an important politician.
   걔는 커서 영향력있는 정치가가 되었어.

A: Paul's dad is very tall. 폴의 아버지는 키가 아주 크셔.

B: I think Paul is going to **grow up to be** tall too.
   폴도 커서 그렇게 클거라고 생각해.

pass up

영영 to choose not to do something, to decline

의미 1.…할 기회를 잡지 못하고 놓치다   2.거절하다

보충 pass up 다음에는 주로 chance, opportunity, offer 등의 단어가 오게 된다.

1. Don't **pass up** your chance to see the world.
   견문을 넓힐 수 있는 기회를 놓치지마

2. You shouldn't **pass up** her offer. 넌 걔의 제안을 놓쳐서는 안돼.

A: Should I take the promotion? 승진을 받아들여야 할까?

B: Never **pass up** a chance for a better job.
   더 좋은 자리로 가는 기회를 절대로 놓치지마.

stay up

> **영영** to remain awake throughout the night without sleeping
>
> **의미** 늦게까지 자지 않다(stay up late), 밤새고 …하다(stay up all night ~ing)
>
> **보충** stay 대신에 be를 써도 된다.

1. She **stayed up** all night working on her presentation.
   걔는 발표회 작업을 하느라 밤을 꼬박 샜어.

2. I **stayed up all night** talking with Jenny about the wedding.
   난 결혼문제로 제니와 밤새 얘기했어.

A: I feel like I want to go to sleep. 자고 싶어.

B: You have to try to **stay up** and study. 자지 않고 공부하도록 해.

turn up

> **영영** to increase the volume; to be found after being sought; to arrive or show up unexpectedly
>
> **의미** 1.어떤 장소에 도착하다, 나타나다   2.(TV 등의 소리) 키우다 ↔ turn down

1. Janis **turned up** at the committee meeting.
   재니스는 위원회에 참석했어.

2. Could you **turn up** the volume of the TV? TV 소리 좀 키워줄래?

A: Why was the room so crowded? 왜 방에 사람들이 가득했던거야?

B: Some unexpected guests **turned up** at the party.
   예상치 못한 손님들이 파티에 나타났어.

look up

영영 to peer upward; to appear to be improving; to research someone or something

의미 1.뭔가에 대한 정보를 찾아보다　2.근처 방문차 겸사해서 들르다, 방문하다　3.…이 좋아지다(상황+be looking up)

보충 look sth up in a dictionary 사전에서 …을 찾아보다. look sth up on the Internet 인터넷에서 찾아보다

1. You should just **look** it **up** on the Internet. It's easy. 인터넷에서 찾아. 쉬워
2. The nation's economy **is looking up** these days. 국가경제가 요즘 좋아지고 있어.

A: What happened to the guy you met on vacation? 휴가 때 만난 남자 어떻게 됐어?

B: He promised to **look** me **up** this summer. 걘 이번 여름에 날 찾아오기로 했어.

come up

영영 to occur or happen; to be discussed; to move to a higher level

의미 1.물리적으로 (다가)가다　2.예기치 않은 일이 생기다　3.다가오다(be coming up)

보충 웨이터나 바텐더가 주로 쓰는 말로 음식 등이 바로 나갑니다라고 할 때 Coming (right) up!이라고 쓴다.

1. **Come up** to my apartment and we'll have a drink together.
   내 아파트로 올라와. 술 같이하자.
2. His birthday's **coming up** soon. 걔의 생일이 곧 다가와.

A: Something's **come up** and he can't attend our wedding.
   일이 생겨서 우리 결혼식에 참석할 수가 없대.

B: That's too bad! 저런!

set up

- **영영** to prepare for something; to trick someone into doing something that could have bad consequences
- **의미** 1.시작(준비)하다 2.설치하다 3.(일정 등을) 정하다 4.누명을 씌우다
- **보충** set up an interview 면접일정을 잡다, set up an appointment 예약을 잡다

1. How long will it take you to **set up**? 설치하는 데 얼마나 걸리나요?
2. I hope that everything **is all set up** by the time we get there.
   난 우리가 도착할 때까지 모든 게 준비 되기를 바래.

A: I'd like to **set up** an appointment for next week.
   다음 주로 약속을 정하고 싶은데요.
B: Tuesday is still open. 화요일은 아직 가능합니다.

fill up

- **영영** to make something full
- **의미** 가득(up) 채우다
- **보충** Fill it['er] up 주유소에서 기름을 가득채우라고 할 때

1. Could you **fill up** my coffee cup? 커피잔을 가득 채워줄래?
2. We stopped to **fill up** the car at the gas station.
   우리는 주유소에서 가득 주유하기 위해 멈췄어.

A: Why didn't you **fill up** the water pitcher? 왜 물주전자에 물을 채워놓지 않았어?
B: I'm sorry, I forgot it was empty. 미안, 비었다는 걸 잊었어.

Unit 01
Unit 02
Unit 03
Unit 04
Unit 05
Unit 06
Unit 07

wake up

영영 to stop sleeping; to cause someone else to stop sleeping

의미 1.일어나다(get up), …을 깨우다(wake sb up)　2.…을 깨닫기 시작하다
(wake up to sth)

보충 wake up call 모닝콜, 경종

1. I hope I didn't **wake** you **up** this morning. 아침잠을 깨운 게 아니겠지.

2. Even though Jim **woke up** late, he caught his bus on time.
비록 짐이 늦잠을 잤지만, 버스를 제 시각에 탔어.

A: I **wake up** at 5 every morning.　난 매일 아침 5시에 일어나.

B: I don't get up as early as you do.　난 너만큼 일찍 일어나지는 않아.

start up

영영 to begin something; to turn on the power to a machine; to
begin a new company or business

의미 1.시작하다, 자동차 시동을 걸다　2.창업하다(start-up company 신생기
업)

보충 start up the company 회사를 창업하다, start up one's own
business 자신의 회사를 세우다

1. Don't **start up** the car until we are inside.
우리가 안으로 들어갈 때까지 차시동을 켜지마.

2. Did you **start up** this restaurant by yourself?
너 혼자 힘으로 이 식당을 시작한거야?

A: No one is willing to invest in the new firm.
아무도 그 새로운 회사에 투자하려고 하지 않아.

B: You can't **start up** a company without money. 돈없이 신생회사를 시작할 수 없어.

pick up

영영 to lift something; to go somewhere in order to give someone a ride

의미 1. 차로 픽업하다   2. 고르다, 사다, (이성을) 낚다   3. (건강, 상황이) 좋아지다

보충 pick up the tab 계산하다, pick up on sth …을 알아차리다

1. We are on our way to the airport to **pick up** the boss.
   우리는 사장님 모시러 공항에 가는 길이야.

2. Did you **pick up** on anything when you were talking to
   Andrew? 너 앤드류에게 얘기할 때 뭔가 알아챘어?

A: Can you **pick up** dinner on the way home? 집에 올 때 저녁 사올 수 있니?

B: No, I don't have time to get it. 아니, 그럴 시간 없어.

clean up

영영 to make a dirty or disorganized area clean and neat; to make a lot of money

의미 1. 치우다, 청소하다   2. 돈을 많이 벌다

보충 clean up the mess 깨끗이 정리하다, get~ cleaned up …을 청소하다

1. Don't forget to **clean** your room. 방청소하는거 잊지마.

2. I'd better **get** these dishes **cleaned up.**
   난 이것들을 설거지 하는게 나을거야.

A: I can't **clean up** this place alone. 나 혼자서는 여기 못 치워.

B: That's why we're here. We'll help you. 그래서 우리가 왔잖아. 우리가 도와줄게.

Unit 01
Unit 02
Unit 03
Unit 04
Unit 05
Unit 06
Unit 07

end up

> **영영** to finish or complete in a certain way
>
> **의미** …로 끝나다, 결국에는 …하게 되다(end up sth[~ing])
>
> **보충** end up with sth 결국 …하게 되다. end in sth…하게 끝이 나다

1. If I get caught, I could **end up** failing the class.
   만일 걸리면, 난 이 수업 낙제하게 될거야.

2. You'll **end up with** a meal no one else wants.
   아무도 원치 않는 식사를 하게 될거야.

A: What kind of phone did you **end up** getting?   결국은 어떤 전화기를 산거니?

B: I got the best of the best.   최고 중에서 최고의 것을 샀지.

make up

> **영영** to invent something that isn't true, to lie; to substitute for something that was cancelled; to reconcile after fighting or arguing
>
> **의미** 1.화장하다(make-up 화장) 2.꾸며대다 3.싸운 후 화해하다

1. He never met the president. He just **made up** that story.
   걔는 사장을 만난 적이 없어. 꾸며낸 이야기였어.

2. Nicole is wearing the ugliest **make-up** I've ever seen.
   니콜은 지금껏 본 것 중 최악의 화장을 하고 있어.

A: I saw you cheating on your girlfriend.   네가 네 여친 몰래 바람피우는거 봤어.

B: That's a lie. Don't **make up** things.   거짓말. 없는 얘기 지어내지마.

split up

> **영영** to divide or break into more than one piece; to separate; to end a relationship
>
> **의미** 주로 남녀관계에서 헤어지다, 이혼하다, 결별하다(split up with sb)
>
> **보충** split up sb (with~)은 …을 (…와) 갈라놓다

1. Melanie **split up with** John last week. 멜라니는 지난주에 존과 헤어졌어.
2. Leslie **split up** Brad **with** his wife.
   레슬리는 브래드가 걔 아내와 헤어지도록 했어.

A: Fran and Bob are always fighting. 프랜과 밥은 늘상 싸워.

B: I'm thinking that they should **split up.** 난 걔네들이 헤어져야 한다고 생각해.

take up

> **영영** to start doing something, especially as a hobby; to occupy space
>
> **의미** 1.시간이나 공간을 잡아먹다, 차지하다 2.취미생활 등을 시작하다
>
> **보충** take up 다음에 시간이나 공간관련 명사가 나온다.

1. The new TV **took up** the whole wall. 새로운 TV는 벽전체를 차지했어.
2. The meeting **took up** three hours. 그 회의는 3시간 걸렸어라고 할 때.

A: The moving truck is enormous. 이삿집 트럭이 엄청나게 크네.

B: It **takes up** several parking spaces. 주차공간 몇자리는 차지하네.

Unit 01
Unit 02
Unit 03
Unit 04
Unit 05
Unit 06
Unit 07

pull up

영영 to use hands to lift something; to drive a vehicle forward

의미 1.신호등에 걸려서 혹은 건물이나 집앞에 차를 세우다   2.의자를 끌고 와서 앉다(pull up a chair)

보충 pull over는 차를 길가에 대다. 사람을 내려주거나 단속에 걸렸을 때.

1. She **pulled up** in front of the gates.   걔는 정문 앞에 차를 세웠어.

2. He **pulled up** a chair to sit down at the table.
   걔는 테이블에 앉기 위해 의자를 가져왔어.

A: Where can we park?   어디에 주차하지?

B: Just **pull up** in the driveway.   주차장 앞에 그냥 대.

go up

영영 to become higher, to rise to a higher place or level

의미 1.물리적으로 올라가다   2.가격이나 주식 등의 수치가 오르다

보충 go down 내려가다. Going up? (엘리베이터) 올라가요?, go up one more floor 한층 더 올라가다

1. Prices of everything will **go up** soon.   모든 것의 가격이 곧 인상될거야.

2. My grades **have gone up** this year.   성적이 금년에 올랐어.

A: Do you want them to **go up** or down?
   그게 오르기를 바라는 거야. 아님 내리기를 바라는 거야?

B: It would be better if they **went down**.   내렸으면 좋겠어.

hang up

영영 to shut off a phone during or after a phone conversation; to impede or stop from moving freely

의미 1.전화를 끊다(get off the phone)　2.통화중에 전화를 끊어버리다(hang up on sb)

보충 예전 미국영화를 보면 전화기가 벽에 걸려 있다. 전화가 오면 수화기를 들어서 통화하다가 끝나면 수화기를 전화기 본체에 건다. 그래서 hang up이라고 쓴다.

1. Please **hang up** the phone. 제발 전화 좀 끊어.
2. Don't **hang up.** Just listen. 전화 끊지 말고 내 얘기 들어.

A: I don't ever want to talk to you again. 다시는 너와 얘기하지 않을거야.

B: Don't **hang up.** Tell me why you're so angry.
전화 끊지마. 왜 그리 화가 났는지 말해 봐.

---

call up

영영 to summon, especially to serve in the military; to contact via the telephone

의미 1.…에게 전화를 걸다(call up sb)　2.전화해서 …하다(call up sb to[and]+V)　3.컴퓨터 화면에 띄우다

보충 call up 부르다, 소집하다

1. **Call up** Tom and tell him we're coming over.
탐에게 전화해서 우리가 가고 있다고 해.

2. I'd like to **call up** Cindy to talk about that.
신디에게 전화해서 그 얘기를 나누고 싶어.

A: I'm planning a party this weekend. 이번 주말에 파티를 열 계획이야.

B: **Call up** some friends and invite them over. 몇몇 친구들에게 전화해서 초대해.

blow up

> **영영** to become very angry suddenly; to explode; to fill with air; to destroy; to make larger
>
> **의미** 1.파괴하다   2.터트리다   3.매우 화를 내다
>
> **보충** blow up in one's face 망신을 톡톡히 당하다

1. How can you be sure it won't **blow up?**
어떻게 그게 폭발하지 않을거라 확신할 수 있어?

2. Unless you want to **blow up,** I'm coming with you.
네가 화내지 않으면 같이 갈게.

A: Did your boyfriend lose his temper? 네 남친이 성질냈어?

B: He **blew up** and everyone felt embarrassed.
화를 많이 내서 다들 당황했어.

throw up

> **영영** to toss into the air; to become sick and vomit
>
> **의미** 1.토하다(throw up on sb)   2.(직장, 도시생활 등을) 집어치우다
>
> **보충** throw up one's hands 두손들다, 포기하다

1. I wish you hadn't seen me **throw up.**
내가 토하는 거 네가 안봤으면 좋을텐데.

2. By the way, it looks like he **threw up** on you.
그나저나, 걔가 너한테 토한 것 같아.

A: I **threw up** during the flight. 비행기 타다 토했어.

B: Flying makes some people sick. 비행기 타면 토하는 사람들이 좀 있어.

Unit 01
Unit 02
Unit 03
Unit 04
Unit 05
Unit 06
Unit 07

back up

영영 to move in a reverse direction; to support or help someone else; to save or put aside something in case of a future problem or emergency

의미 1.지원하다 2.컴퓨터 백업하다 3.(차량) 후진하다 4.뒤로 물러서다

보충 back up on one's feet 재기하다

1. Let's **back up**! Give her some room here!
   잠시 물러서세요! 걔한테 길 좀 비켜주세요!

2. Luckily, I had my friends to **back** me **up**.
   다행히도, 내 친구들이 나를 지원해줬어.

A: Did Steve tell people you were being honest?
   스티브가 사람들에게 네가 정직했다고 말했어?

B: Yeah, he **backed up** everything I said. 어, 내가 말한 모든 내용이 맞다고 해줬어.

act up

영영 to behave in a rude or bad way; to cease to function correctly

의미 1.버릇없이 굴다 2.작동이 멈추다, 고장나다, 기계가 말을 안듣다

1. Tell your kid to stop **acting up**. 네 아이에게 그만 버릇없이 굴라고 해.

2. It's a good car, but it **acts up** sometimes. 차는 좋은데 가끔 말을 안들어.

A: My phone **is acting up**. Can I borrow yours?
   내 폰이 말을 안듣네. 네 것 좀 빌려줘.

B: Sure, call whoever you want. 그래, 누구한테든 전화해.

Unit 01
Unit 02
Unit 03
Unit 04
Unit 05
Unit 06
Unit 07

build up

> **영영** to make bigger or stronger; to improve a reputation; to improve a person's confidence
>
> **의미** 1.더 크고 강하게 만들다 2.명성을 높이다, 자신감을 제고하다

1. The city plans to **build up** itself as a tourist destination.
도시는 관광지로 조성할 계획이야.

2. It took years for me to **build up** this muscle.
이 근육을 만들기 위해 수년이 걸렸어.

A: How did you **build up** your company? 어떻게 네 회사를 키운거야?

B: It took a lot of time and hard work. 많은 시간과 열심히 노력한 결과야.

cover up

> **영영** to put something over another thing so it can't be seen; to try to hide wrongdoing or illegal actions
>
> **의미** 은폐하다(get sb covered)
>
> **보충** cover-up 은폐

1. I don't have anything to **cover up.** I like Chris.
난 숨길게 하나도 없어. 난 크리스를 좋아해.

2. You're making up new lies to **cover up** the old ones.
넌 지난 거짓말을 숨기기 위해 새로운 거짓말을 꾸며내고 있어.

A: They found he'd been cheating on his wife.
걔가 자기 부인 몰래 바람피고 있었다는게 밝혀졌어.

B: He'd been **covering** it **up** for many years. 걔는 그걸 오랫동안 숨기고 있었어.

dress up

영영 to make something look better; to put on formal clothing

의미 성장하다, 잘 차려입다 ↔ dress down 편안하게 옷을 입다

보충 dress up for sb …을 위해 차려입다.

1. I can't believe you're **dressing up** for him.
   걔 때문에 이렇게까지 차려 입다니.

2. Some new furniture will **dress up** your apartment.
   몇몇 새로운 가구로 네 아파트는 새단장하게 될 거야.

A: Why **are** you **dressing up** today? 오늘 왜 그렇게 차려 입었어?

B: I have a date with a beautiful woman. 아름다운 여인과 데이트가 있어.

hold up

영영 to delay or not allow to continue; to rob using a weapon; to raise into the air

의미 1.지탱하다, 버티다 2.총으로 위협하여 강탈하다(holdup 노상강도) 3.미루다(holdup 지체)

보충 be[get] held up …에 꼼짝 못하게 잡히다. **What's the hold up?** 왜 이리 늦는거야?

1. What's **the hold up** with your homework? It's late!
   숙제 왜 이리 늦는거야? 늦었어!

2. I **got held up** behind a traffic accident. 교통사고에 꼼짝 못하게 잡혔어.

A: Sorry, but my brother is going to be late. 미안하지만 내 형이 늦을거야.

B: He's **holding up** the entire group. 네 형 때문에 다들 못가고 있잖아.

screw up

영영 to make a big mistake that causes problems

의미 일을 망치다, …을 망쳤어(screw sth up; screw up sth)

보충 screwup 실수, 바보

1. I'm not going to let you **screw** it **up** now.
네가 이걸 망치도록 가만히 두지 않을거야.

2. I **screwed up** again. I just can't seem to finish this drawing!
또 망쳤네. 이 그림을 영영 끝낼 수 없을 것 같아!

A: Ted downloaded some kind of Internet virus.
테드는 뭔가 인터넷 바이러스를 다운로드했어.

B: He really **screwed up** the computer. 걘 정말이지 컴퓨터를 망쳐버렸구나.

mess up

영영 to do something incorrectly, to make a mistake

의미 1.엉망으로 만들다, 망치다   2.실수하다(Sb screws up (sth))

보충 You messed up 네가 망쳐놓았어

1. You **mess up,** and you're going to prison.
네가 잘못했고 감방에 갈거야.

2. She can **mess up** our lives for a couple of weeks.
걘 몇 주안에 우리 삶을 망칠 수 있어.

A: The virus came from a website. 바이러스가 한 웹사이트에서 침투한거야.

B: How does it **mess up** a computer? 그게 어떻게 컴퓨터를 엉망으로 만드는거야?

hit sb up

> 영영 to tell someone to call or make contact with you
> 의미 페이스북 등 SNS 및 전화 등으로 연락을 하다

1. **Hit** me **up** on Facebook when you get a chance.
시간되면 페이스북으로 연락해.

2. I told Sarah to **hit** me **up** this afternoon.
난 새라에게 오늘 오후에 연락하라고 했어.

A: I can't talk, I have lots of work to do. 난 말할 시간없어, 할 일이 너무 많아.

B: OK, **hit** me **up** when you get finished. 알았어. 끝나고 연락해.

live up

> 영영 to spend time doing whatever is most enjoyable or fun, often spending a lot of money
> 의미 1.충족시키다, 부응하다(live up to~) 2.신나게 돈쓰며 즐기다(live it up)
> 보충 live up to one's expectations …의 기대에 부응하다

1. We're trying to **live up** to our word.
우린 우리가 한 말을 지키며 살려고 해.

2. **Live it up** before you get married. 결혼하기 전에 신나게 놀아.

A: That was a wild party. 아주 신나는 파티였어.

B: Yeah, I like to **live it up.** 어, 신나게 돈쓰는 것을 좋아해.

Unit 01
Unit 02
Unit 03
Unit 04
Unit 05
Unit 06
Unit 07

be tied up

> **영영** to be busy or unavailable; to be physically restrained by ropes or cords
>
> **의미** 묶여 있을 정도로 꼼짝달싹 못하게 바쁘다(be tied up with[~ing])
>
> **보충** live up to one's expectations …의 기대에 부응하다

1. **I've been tied up** all day in the office.
   사무실에서 하루 종일 꼼짝달싹 못했어.

2. **I got a little tied up** with work. 일로 좀 많이 바빴어.

A: When can I stop by to pick up the computer?
   언제 그 컴퓨터를 가지러 들르면 될까?

B: Well, I'm **kind of tied up** all day. How about tomorrow?
   그런데 말야, 내가 오늘 하루 온종일 바빠서 꼼짝도 못할 것같아. 내일 들르는 게 어때?

get worked up

> **영영** to become angry, excited or upset
>
> **의미** 1.흥분하다   2.폭빠지다(be worked up)
>
> **보충** work sb up은 …의 감정을 고조시키다

1. Every time he **gets worked up,** he yells at us.
   걘 화가날 때마다 우리에게 소리를 질러

2. Bob really **got worked up** when he went to the rock concert.
   락 콘서트에 가자 밥은 정말 흥분했었어.

A: How did Chris react when Jill broke up with him?
   질이 헤어지자고 했을 때 크리스의 반응은 어땠어?

B: He **got worked up.** He couldn't believe it. 열받았지. 믿기지 않는 듯 했어.

catch up with

- **영영** to come to the same place as someone or something that is ahead; to discuss life events with someone that had been out of contact
- **의미** 1.(일이나 부족한 것을) 따라잡다, 만나다 2.자리에 없던 사람에게 무슨 일이 있었는지 새로운 소식 등을 말해주다
- **보충** catch sb up on~ …에게 …대해 말해주다, catch up with later 나중에 보다

1. There was no time to **catch up with** the others.
   다른 사람들을 따라잡을 시간이 없었어.

2. Please **catch** me **up on** what you are doing. 너 어떻게 지내는지 말해봐.

A: I have to leave right away for the meeting. 회의가 있어 당장 가봐야겠어.

B: I'll **catch up with** you later. 나중에 다시 보자.

mix up with

- **영영** to confuse, to misunderstand; to get the details of several things wrong
- **의미** 혼동하다 = get mixed up
- **보충** mix-up 혼동으로 야기된 실수나 문제

1. Our reservation **was mixed up with** another guest.
   우리 예약이 다른 손님꺼와 혼동됐어

2. You weren't invited because of **a mix-up.**
   넌 실수로 초대를 받지 못했어.

A: Why weren't you at the meeting? 너 왜 회의에 참석하지 않았어?

B: I **mixed up** that time **with** another meeting. 다른 미팅시간과 혼동했어.

Unit 01

Unit 02

Unit 03

Unit 04

Unit 05

Unit 06

Unit 07

be fed up with

영영 to be frustrated or upset at someone or because of a situation

의미 질리다, 싫증나다 = get sick of~

보충 ~ing가 이어질 때는 be fed up with ~ing 혹은 be fed up ~ing로 with 를 생략해 써도 된다.

1. **I'm totally fed up with** her behavior. 난 걔의 행동에 넌더리가 나.

2. **I got sick of** waiting for him. 난 걔를 기다리는데 질렸어.

A: Why are Jack and Brooke fighting? 왜 잭하고 브룩이 싸우는거야?

B: Brooke **is fed up with** Jack's behavior. 브룩이 잭의 행동에 넌더리가 났대.

break up with

영영 to end a relationship with a romantic partner

의미 사귀다가 헤어지다

보충 on a break는 사귀는 도중 잠시 헤어진 기간을 말한다.

1. It looks like she's going to **break up with** Tom.
   걔는 탐과 헤어질 것 같아.

2. Josie **broke up with** the guy she was dating.
   조시는 데이트하던 남자와 헤어졌어.

A: I heard you had some trouble with your girlfriend.
   너 여친하고 문제가 좀 있다며.

B: I had to **break up with** her. We were fighting a lot.
   난 걔와 헤어져야 했어. 우린 많이 싸웠거든.

hook up with

영영 to give something or introduce someone or put a person in contact with another person; (hook up) to have a casual sexual encounter

의미 1. …을 주거나 소개시켜주다, …와 섹스하다   2. …와 섹스하다(hook up의 경우)

보충 hook up은 실제 요즘 현실에서는 거의 섹스와 관련되어서 쓰인다고 보면 된다.

1. If you're going to be in LA, I'll **hook** you **up with** my brother.
LA에 갈거라면 내 동생을 소개시켜줄게.

2. You're pissed 'cause I **hooked up with** your friend.
내가 네 친구하고 자니까 열받았지.

A: Why are you staring at that woman? 왜 저 여자를 쳐다보는거야?

B: I think I **hooked up with** her a few months ago. 몇달 전에 섹스했던 여자같아.

set up with

영영 to arrange for two people to get together for a date

의미 데이트하도록 두명을 연결[소개]시켜 주다

보충 set 대신에 fix를 써도 된다.

1. I can't believe I **set** you **up with** such a monster!
내가 너한테 그런 괴물같은 놈을 소개시켜주다니!

2. I **set** her **up with** one of my cousins.
난 걔를 내 사촌 중 한 명에게 소개시켜줬어.

A: Can you **set** me **up with** one of your friends? 네 친구 한 명 소개시켜주라.

B: Most of my friends are already married. 친구들 거의 다 결혼했어.

keep up with

영영 to maintain the same speed or capability as another; to stay aware of new developments, to be aware of the most recent news

의미 1.뒤떨어지지 않다, 따라잡다   2.연락하고 지내다   3.…을 잘 알고 있다

보충 with 다음에는 sb나 sth이 온다.

1. The new student couldn't **keep up with** the others.
그 전학생은 다른 친구들을 따라잡을 수가 없었어.

2. I'm sure he can't **keep up with** you. 걔가 널 따라갈 수 없다고 확신해.

A: Fred and Sue just bought a big yacht. 프레드와 수는 큰 요트를 구입했어.

B: You'll never be able to **keep up with** your rich friends.
넌 절대로 네 부자친구들을 따라잡지 못할거야.

come up with

영영 to produce or be able to present something that is needed

의미 1.좋은 생각이나 계획 등을 생각해내다   2.구실이나 변명을 생각해내다

보충 come up with + money 돈을 마련하다, 제공하다

1. We'd better **come up with** a good plan soon!
우리는 아주 좋은 계획을 곧 생각해내야 돼!

2. Let me see what you'**ve come up with.** 어떤 안을 내놓았는지 한번 보자.

A: I have no idea where I'll be sleeping tonight.
오늘밤 어디서 자야될지 모르겠어.

B: You'd better **come up with** something quick.
빨리 뭔가 생각을 해내야겠다.

put up with

영영 to endure or tolerate, especially when it is something that is unpleasant

의미 인내심을 발휘하고 참고 받아들이다, 짜증나는 상황이나 사람을 참다

보충 with 다음에는 sb[sth]이 온다. put up with sb ~ing하게 되면 …가 …하는 것을 참다.

1. We just **put up with** it because we love you.
   우리는 너를 사랑하기 때문에 그걸 참아냈어.

2. You have to **put up with** her making noise. 걔가 시끄럽게 하는 걸 참아야 해.

A: Why did Justin divorce his wife? 왜 저스틴은 아내와 이혼했어?

B: He couldn't **put up with** all the arguing. 허구헌날 다툼질에 참을 수가 없었어.

make up for

영영 to substitute or compensate for something that was expected but not delivered

의미 밀린 것 혹은 상대방에게 끼친 피해 등을 보상하다

보충 make it up to sb …에게 보상하다

1. We'll **make up for** the missed class next week.
   우리는 다음주에 빠진 수업을 보충할거야.

2. I forgot your birthday, but I'll **make it up to** you.
   네 생일을 깜빡했지만 보상해줄게.

A: He'll have to **make up for** the time he's been away.
   그 사람은 자기가 비운 시간을 보충해야 할거야.

B: He said he'll **make it up** this weekend.
   그 사람 얘기가 이번 주에 자기가 못한 시간만큼 일을 하겠대.

Unit 01
Unit 02
Unit 03
Unit 04
Unit 05
Unit 06
Unit 07

stand up for

영영 to support someone or something, especially when it is not popular

의미 불리한 상황에 있는 것을 지지하다, 옹호하다

보충 stand up to sb 부당한 대우를 하는 사람에게 맞서다

1. I need you to **stand up for** me the next time.
다음 번엔 당신이 내 편을 들어줬으면 좋겠어

2. Nick always **stands up for** his friends. 닉은 언제나 자기 친구들을 옹호해.

A: I heard someone wanted to fight you. 어떤 사람이 너와 겨루고 싶다며.

B: Yes, but my friends **stood up for** me. 어, 하지만 내 친구들이 나를 지지했어.

sign up for

영영 to agree to do something; to legally promise, via a contract, to take a job or do a type of work

의미 특정 강좌에 등록하거나 조직에 들어가다, 가입하다

보충 회사나, 군대 혹은 클럽에 가입할 때도 쓴다.

1. I **signed up for** the new Internet service.
난 새로운 인터넷 서비스 강좌에 등록했어.

2. They went to **sign up for** the debate club.
걔네들은 토론클럽에 가입하러 갔어.

A: Do you have plans for this summer? 이번 여름에 무슨 계획있어?

B: I'm going to **sign up for** some English classes. 영어강좌에 등록할려고.

stick up for

영영 to defend someone, especially when others are being unkind or fighting with the person

의미 비난받는 편을 들어주다, 변호하다, 옹호하다

보충 stick up 손을 들다, 총을 이용해 은행이나 사람을 털다

1. He didn't even **stick up for** me. 걘 내 편을 들어주지도 않았어.

2. She didn't even **stick up for** me when people were being unkind. 사람들이 내게 불친절한데도 내 편을 들어주지 않았어.

A: It seems that you are very close to your brother.
   넌 네 오빠와 아주 가까운 것 같아.

B: He **stuck up for** me when I was growing up.
   내가 자랄 때 내 편을 들어줬어.

be up to

영영 to be doing something; to be the most something can be; to be well enough or strong enough to do something

의미 1.…하는 중이다 2.꾸미다 3.…을 할 수 있다

보충 be up to sb …에 달려있다

1. What **are** you **up to** next week at this time?
   다음주 이 시간엔 뭐할거야?

2. I'm going to find out what my husband **is up to.**
   내 남편이 뭘 꾸미고 있는지 알아낼거야.

A: Well Chris, what **have** you **been up to**? 어 크리스, 그간 어떻게 지냈어?

B: I went on a summer vacation with my parents this year.
   금년에 부모님하고 여름휴가 갔었어.

come up against

영영 to face opposition; to face difficulty or the need to do a difficult task

의미 직면하다, 부딪히다, 대항하다

1. They **came up against** strong winds when they climbed the mountain. 걔네들은 등산할 때 강풍에 직면했어.

2. You'll **come up against** many difficulties in life.
   넌 살면서 많은 어려움에 직면하게 될거야.

A: So they never got married? 그래서 걔네들 결혼 못한거야?

B: No, they **came up against** problems in their relationship.
   했어. 사귀면서 생기는 문제들을 극복했어.

calm down

영영 to relax or become less upset

의미 고조된 감정을 가라앉히다, 진정하다, (사물주어) 상황이 진정되다

보충 calm sb down …을 진정시키다

1. Sweetie, **calm down,** it's going to be okay.
   자기야, 진정해. 괜찮을거야.

2. What can I do to **calm** everyone **down?**
   모두를 진정시키기 위해 어떻게 해야 할까?

A: Okay, let's...let's all just **calm down** here. 좋아. 다들 진정하자고.

B: All right...I'll be in the waiting room. 그래. 난 대기실에 있을게.

sit down

- **영영** to be seated after standing
- **의미** 자리에 앉다
- **보충** sit down and+V 앉아서 …하다, take[have] a seat 자리에 앉다

1. I'm starving and I can't wait to **sit down** and eat lunch.
   배고파 미칠 지경이야. 앉아서 점심 먹고 싶어 죽겠어

2. **Take a seat.** The doctor will see you soon.
   자리에 앉아요. 의사선생님이 곧 진찰하실겁니다.

A: I'd like to see Mr. Franks. 프랭크 씨를 만나고 싶어요.

B: **Sit down** and I'll find him for you. 앉아계시면 제가 찾아볼게요.

slow down

- **영영** to make something go slower; to delay
- **의미** 1.천천히 하다, 속도를 줄이다   2.연기하다
- **보충** slow up 속도를 줄이다

1. You've got to **slow down** when you drive.
   넌 운전할 때 속도를 줄여야 돼.

2. **Slow up** a little! I can't keep up with you.
   좀 천천히 가! 못따라가겠어.

A: Why don't you **slow down** a bit? 좀 천천히 가자.

B: I like to drive fast. 난 빨리 달리는 걸 좋아해.

cut down (on)

> **영영** to reduce the amount of something that is used
>
> **의미** 비용, 경비, 술, 담배 등을 예전보다 줄이다
>
> **보충** cut back on sth 건강을 위해서 줄이다

1. You have to **cut down on** spending. 넌 돈쓰는 것 좀 줄여야 돼.

2. I **cut back on** coffee after my heart attack.
   난 심장마비가 온 후에 커피를 줄였어.

A: Money has been tight. 자금이 빡빡해.

B: We have to **cut down on** our purchases. 물건 사는 것들을 줄여야 돼.

turn down

> **영영** to say no to something, to refuse; to move something downward
>
> **의미** 1.상대방의 제의나 제안을 거절하다   2.(소리 등) 줄이다   3.…을 밑으로 이동하다
>
> **보충** 소리 등을 키우다는 turn up

1. I decided to **turn down** the promotion. 난 승진을 거절하기로 했어.

2. Can you **turn down** the volume on the TV? TV소리 좀 줄여 줄래?

A: What are you going to do with the offer? 그 제안을 어떻게 할거야?

B: I'm pretty sure I'm going to **turn** it **down**. 거절하게 될 게 분명해.

Unit 01
Unit 02
Unit 03
Unit 04
Unit 05
Unit 06
Unit 07

go down

영영 to occur; to sink or go lower; to move to a lower height; (slang) to happen

의미 1.떨어지다 2.(계단, 수치 등) 내려가다, 줄다 3.…로 (내려)가다 = go down to~

보충 Going up or down? (엘리베이터) 올라가나요, 내려가나요?

1. **Go down** this street and turn to the left. 이 길로 쭉 간 다음 좌회전하세요.

2. The price of gasoline **is going down.** 휘발유 가격이 내려가고 있어.

A: Can I get you something to drink? 뭐 좀 마실 것 갖다 줄까?

B: Yeah, **go down** and get me some coffee. 어, 가서 커피 좀 사다 줘.

break down

영영 to stop working correctly; to have a sudden serious psychological problem; to reduce to smaller pieces; to carefully explain something

의미 1.기계나 차량 등이 고장나다 2.신경이 쇠약해지다 3.알아듣기 쉽게 설명하다

보충 shut down 가게, 회사 등이 망해서 문닫다, 컴퓨터 끄다

1. I couldn't come because my car **broke down.**
   차가 고장나서 올 수 없었어.

2. He **shut down** his computer and cleared his desk.
   걘 컴퓨터를 끄고 책상을 깨끗이 치웠어.

A: Did your car **break down** again? 네 차 또 고장났어?

B: It did, and that's the third time in two weeks. 응. 두 주 동안 이번이 세 번째야.

get down to

영영 to arrive at the end of something; to begin the most important part; to start working

의미 1.도착하다 2.(내려)가다 3.to 이하의 일을 진지하게 많은 노력을 기울이며 시작하다

보충 get down to work 일에 착수하다, get down to business 일에 본격적으로 착수하다, 본론으로 들어가다

1. You need to **get down to** the heart of the matter.
   문제의 핵심에 집중해야 돼.

2. What're you doing here? **Get down to** the OR right now.
   여기서 뭐해? 수술실로 바로 가.

A: We need to **get down to** work. 본격적으로 일을 착수할 필요가 있겠어.

B: Just let me finish my lunch and we can start. 점심마저 먹고 시작하면 돼.

settle down

영영 to become calm, to stop behaving in an excited manner; to lead a quieter life, especially after marrying and having a family

의미 1.진정하다 2.결혼하고 아기를 갖는 등 차분하게 정착하다

1. **Settle down,** we need everyone to be quiet!
   진정해, 우리 모두가 조용히해야 돼!

2. We **settled down** in a suburb of Chicago. 우린 시카고 외곽에 정착했어.

A: I'm worried that my sister acts too wild.
   내 여동생이 너무 거칠게 행동하는지 걱정돼.

B: She will **settle down** when she gets older. 나이들면서 차분해질거야.

fall down

영영 to drop to the ground; to fail to do what is expected

의미 1.넘어지다, 무너지다   2.(옷 등이) 흘러내리다

보충 fall down the stairs 계단에서 넘어지다

1. My mother **fell down** the stairs the other day.
   어머니가 요전 날 계단에서 떨어지셨어.

2. Don't hurry. You may **fall down** and hurt yourself.
   서두르지 마. 넘어져 다칠 수도 있어.

A: Why isn't the TV working anymore? 왜 TV가 안되는거야?

B: It **fell down** and shattered the screen. 떨어져서 화면이 깨졌어.

let down

영영 to disappoint, to not do what was promised or expected

의미 기대와 예상을 벗어나 실망시키다 = disappoint

보충 Don't let me down 날 실망시키지마, I won't let you down again 다시는 널 실망시키지 않을게

1. You **let me down.** I thought I could trust you.
   너 때문에 실망했어. 난 널 믿을 수 있다고 생각했는데.

2. Your mother will **be very disappointed to** hear that.
   네 엄마는 그 소식을 듣고 매우 실망하실거야.

A: You have to work hard. Don't **let me down.**
   열심히 일 해야 돼. 날 실망시키지마.

B: I'll do my best, boss. Believe me. 사장님, 최선을 다할게요. 믿으세요.

back down

영영 to admit to being wrong; to withdraw from a confrontation

의미 1.잘못을 인정하다　2.주장을 굽히다　3.포기하다, 철회하다

1. And now you're telling me to back down?
   이제와서 나보고 물러서라고 말하는거야?

2. If you don't back down, there's going to be a fight.
   네가 물러서지 않으면 싸움이 벌어질거야.

A: So your husband is still mad at you?　그래 네 남편 아직도 너한테 화나 있니?

B: When he gets angry, he never backs down.
   그이는 화나면 절대 물러서는 적이 없어.

close down

영영 to not allow something to continue; to stop from doing business; to stay until a business closes, especially while drinking alcohol

의미 1.가게 문을 닫다, 폐쇄하다　2.술집 문 닫을 때까지 마시다

1. I'm closing down my office. I've lost all my clients.
   사무실 문을 닫을거야. 모든 고객을 잃었어.

2. I can't just close down the shop. I've got customers.
   손님들이 있어 가게 문 못 닫아요.

A: You look terrible this morning.　너 오늘 아주 안좋아 보인다.

B: I closed down a bar with a friend of mine.
   내 친구 한 명과 가게 문 닫을 때까지 바에서 술마셨어.

write down

> 영영 to put information on a piece of paper
> 의미 기록하다, 적다

1. **Write down** this information so you don't forget.
잊어버리지 않도록 이 정보 적어놔.

2. The reporter is going to **write down** what is said.
기자가 발언들을 적어놓을거야.

A: Want me to pick up anything at the store? 가게가서 뭐 사올까?

B: I'll **write down** the things I need. 내가 필요한거 적을게.

run down

> 영영 to overtake; to become worn out, fatigued or tired; to find or gather specific information; to insult or criticize someone; to run out of energy and be unable to function
> 의미 1.뛰어내려가다 2.닳아지다, 지치다 3.특정 정보를 찾아내다 4.비난하다 5.고장나다
> 보충 run(-)down 낡아빠진, 피곤한

1. I'll have Sam **run down** the gun's serial number.
샘보고 총의 시리얼넘버를 찾아내라고 할거야.

2. I've been feeling **a little run down** lately. 난 최근에 좀 지쳤어.

A: Have you ever **felt run down**? 몹시 피곤한 적이 있어?

B: I've been **exhausted** since I became a father.
아기가 태어난 이후로 아주 지쳤어.

put down

영영 to insult or intentionally make someone feel bad

의미 1.기록하다 2.내려놓다 3.전화끊다 4.진정[압]시키다 5.비난하다

보충 단순하게 물리적으로 내려놓다라고도 쓰인다.

1. I can't believe you put me down in front of your friend!
   네가 네 친구들 앞에서 날 어떻게 깔봐!

2. I pay one hundred dollars for dinner, you put down twenty.
   난 저녁값으로 100달러를 내는데 넌 20달러를 내놓는구만.

A: That guy is an idiot, he's really stupid. 저 녀석은 바보야, 정말 멍청하다고.

B: A lot of people put him down. 많은 사람들이 걔를 비난했어.

crack down on

영영 to make a strong effort to stop something bad or illegal, particularly when the police try to stop an illegal activity

의미 1.경찰 등이 불법집회를 진압하다, 단속하다 2.조치를 취하다

1. The cops are cracking down on pick pockets.
   경찰이 소매치기들을 제압하고 있어.

2. Teachers plan to crack down on students who cheat.
   교사들은 부정행위하는 학생들을 단속할 계획이야.

A: There are too many people begging for money.
   돈을 구걸하는 사람들이 너무 많아.

B: It's time that the police crack down on them.
   경찰들이 조치를 취해야 할 때야.

look down on

> **영영** to consider something to be inferior or not as good; to view from a higher point
>
> **의미** 1.내려다보다 2.멸시하다, 경멸하다
>
> **보충** 반대는 look up to sb

1. Most rich people **look down on** others.
   대부분의 부유층은 다른 사람들을 무시해.

2. Never **look down on** honest work. 힘들고 정직한 일을 깔봐서는 안돼.

A: I'd really love to date Arianna. 난 정말이지 아리안나와 데이트하고 싶어.

B: Forget it pal, she **looks down on** you. 친구야, 잊어라. 걘 널 무시해.

come down with

> **영영** to suddenly become sick
>
> **의미** 주로 가벼운 병에 걸리다(develop)
>
> **보충** come down with+illness (not disease) *develop 다음에는 중병도 온다.

1. Our teacher **came down with** the flu. 우리 선생님은 독감에 걸렸어.

2. I think I'm just **coming down** with a migraine. 편두통이 오는 것 같아.

A: Where's Randy today? 오늘 빌은 어디 있니?

B: He **came down with** a cold and called in sick.
   그 친구 감기에 걸려서 병가냈어.

for·of·on

for
…을 향해, 동안, 자격 ex. search for, last for

of
원인, 이유, 관련, 관계 ex. die of, think of

on
…에, …와 동시에, 시기, 의존

ex. fall on, count on

look for

> **영영** to seek someone or something
> **의미** 뭔가 필요한 사람이나 사물을 구하거나 원하는 것을 찾다

1. **Are** you **looking for** anything in particular?
   뭔가 특별한 거를 찾고 있나요?

2. Chris needs to go **look for** a new job.
   크리스는 새로운 직업을 찾아봐야 해.

A: I cannot meet my friend without arguing with him.
   난 친구랑 만나면 꼭 다툰단 말야.

B: Maybe you should **look for** new friends. 새로운 친구들을 찾아봐.

wait for

> **영영** to stay until someone or something arrives or is ready
> **의미** 사물이나 사람을 기다리다
> **보충** wait for sb to+V …가 …하기를 기다리다, wait until[till] S+V …할 때까지 기다리다

1. We'll **wait for** you to get back before we start.
   네가 돌아오는거 기다렸다가 시작할게.

2. I'll **be waiting for** you in the living room. 거실에서 기다릴게.

A: Could you **wait for** me in my office? 사무실에 가서 날 기다려주겠니?

B: Sure. I'll go and make myself comfortable.
   알았어. 내가 가서 편안하게 있을게.

work for

영영 to be employed by; to labor for a specific goal; to be effective

의미 1. …에서 일하다   2. 효과가 있다

보충 work for+사람[회사], work for the government 공무원이다

1. Which manager do you **work for?**   어떤 부장 밑에서 일하는거야?
2. I **work for** a small company.   나는 조그만 회사에 다녀.

A: I wish I could **work for** the government.   공무원이면 좋겠어.

B: It's a stable job but not very exciting.   안정적이기는 하지만 신나지는 않잖아.

care for

영영 to feel affection for someone; to protect the health or well being of someone or something

의미 1. (긍정 평서문) 돌보다   2. 좋아하다   3. (부정문, 의문문) 좋아하다, 원하다

보충 not care to+V …하고 싶지 않다, Would you care to~? …하겠어요?

1. You had to **care for** your family.   넌 네 가족을 돌봐야했어
2. You have no idea what it's like to **care for** somebody.
   다른 누군가를 좋아한다는게 뭔지 너는 몰라.

A: Willie and Sheila spend a lot of time together.
   윌리와 쉴라는 함께 시간을 많이 보내.

B: I think they **care for** each other.   서로 좋아하는 것 같아.

ask for

- **영영** to make a request for something
- **의미** 1.요청하다, 요구하다 2.…을 묻다, 물어보다
- **보충** You asked for it! 네가 자초한 일이야!

1. I need to **ask for** your help again. 또 다시 너한테 도움을 청해야겠어.
2. I would like to **ask for** your advice about something.
   어떤 일에 대해서 조언을 구하고 싶어.

A: I need to **ask for** some help here. 이것 좀 도와줘야겠는데.
B: You name it. What can I do for you? 말해 봐. 뭘 도와줘야 하지?

beg for

- **영영** to strongly plead to have something
- **의미** 간청하다, 애원하다
- **보충** beg to+V …하기를 간청하다, beg sb not to+V …에게 …하지 말아달라고 간청하다

1. There's no need to **beg for** extra help. 추가 도움을 청할 필요가 없어.
2. I'm ashamed about **begging for** money. 돈을 빌려달라고 해서 창피해.

A: What did Ted do after he was fired? 테드는 해고된 후에 어떻게 했어?
B: He **begged for** his old job back. 걘 일을 계속하게 해달라고 간청했어.

leave for

영영 to depart for another place; to depart without offering assistance; to break up with a romantic partner in favor of another person

의미 1.…을 향해 출발하다, 도움없이 출발하다   2.다른 사람이 생겨서 애인과 헤어지다

보충 leave for+장소 …을 향해 출발하다, leave+장소 …을 떠나다, 나가다

1. They are preparing to **leave for** the wedding.
   걔네들은 결혼식장에 갈 준비를 하고 있어.

2. Jane wants to **leave for** New York before you change your mind. 제인은 네가 맘을 바꾸기 전에 뉴욕으로 출발하기를 원해.

A: Why are you packing suitcases? 왜 짐가방을 싸고 있어?

B: I need to **leave for** Tokyo in the morning. 오늘 아침에 도쿄로 출발해야 돼.

fall for

영영 to be fooled or tricked; to fall in love with someone

의미 1.속아 넘어가다(fall for sth)   2.홀딱 반하다(fall for sb)

1. Don't **fall for** the sweet things she says.
   걔가 하는 달콤한 말에 넘어가지마.

2. I **fell for** Chris shortly after we met.
   난 우리가 만난 후에 크리스에게 홀딱 반했어.

A: How did your mom lose so much money?
   네 엄마는 어쩌다 그렇게 많은 돈을 잃었어?

B: She **fell for** some investment scam. 엄마는 투자사기에 속아넘어갔어.

stand for

> **영영** to symbolize something; to support a position or opinion
> **의미** 1.상징하다, 뜻하다 2.(특정한 원칙이나 가치) 지원하다, 편들다
> **보충** not stand for[to+V] …을[…하는 것을] 참지 못하다

1. He won't **stand for** such poor treatment.
   걘 그런 허접한 대접을 받아들이지 않을거야.

2. Our club **stands for** hard work and honesty.
   우리 클럽은 근면과 정직을 지지해.

A: Why do churches have crosses on them? 왜 교회에는 십자가가 있는거야?
B: They **stand for** the Christian religion. 십자가는 기독교를 상징하잖아.

search for

> **영영** to seek in order to find something or someone
> **의미** 자기가 필요로 하는 사물이나 사람을 찾다
> **보충** 인터넷을 검색하다는 do a search 혹은 do research on the Internet

1. The cops need to **search for** the prisoners.
   경찰들은 탈옥한 죄수들을 찾아야 돼.

2. I'm still **searching for** my phone. 난 아직도 내 핸드폰을 찾고 있어.

A: Can I help you? 찾으시는거 있으세요?
B: I'm **searching for** a good novel. 좋은 소설을 찾고 있어요.

prepare for

영영 to get ready for something; to anticipate a future event

의미 …할 준비를 하다 = prepare to+V

보충 prepare food 음식을 준비하다, prepare a report 보고서를 준비하다

1. Then **be prepared to** suffer the consequences.
   그럼 결과를 받아들일 준비를 해.

2. I have to **prepare for** a big examination tomorrow.
   내일 있을 중요한 시험을 준비해야 돼.

A: Why do you have these books? 왜 이 책들을 갖고 있는거야?

B: I'm **preparing to** enter medical school. 의대 들어갈 준비를 하고 있어.

apply for

영영 to make a formal written request for something

의미 (학교, 직장 등에) 지원하다, 신청하다

보충 apply sth to~ …을 …에 (크림, 로션) 바르다

1. How can I **apply for** a visa? 비자신청을 어떻게 해?

2. I would like to **apply for** the position in advertising.
   광고에 난 자리에 지원하고 싶은데요.

A: Where can I **apply for** a job? 어디서 입사지원을 하나요?

B: Go to that office over there. 저쪽 사무실로 가세요.

apologize for

> **영영** to express regret, to say you're sorry
> **의미** 자기가 한 행동에 대해 사과하다(apologize for+N[~ing])
> **보충** apologize to sb …에게 사과하다

1. I was just coming over here to **apologize for** my behavior!
   내 행동을 사과하려고 여기 왔다구!

2. He will not go **apologize to** her. 걘 가서 그녀에게 사과를 하지 않을거야.

A: I'm sorry, but I don't know what to say.
   미안하지만 뭐라 해야 할 지 모르겠어.

B: Maybe you should **apologize to** me. 내게 사과해야지.

pay for

> **영영** to give money to buy something
> **의미** …에 대한 비용을 치르다
> **보충** pay sb for sth …에게 …의 비용을 내다, pay+돈 for sth …사는데 돈을 지불하다

1. Can I **pay for** the parking when I leave? 나갈 때 주차비를 내면 되나요?

2. I paid a hundred dollars **for** them. 그것들 사는데 백달러 들었어.

A: Sam wants me to **pay for** the entire vacation.
   샘은 내가 휴가내내 비용을 대기를 원해.

B: Why should you **pay for** everything? 왜 네가 모든 비용을 내야 하는데?

head for

> **영영** to move in the direction of something
>
> **의미** 특정 방향을 향해 가다(head for, head towards)
>
> **보충** be headed to, be headed off to 역시 …로 향하다. Where are you headed?는 어디가?

1. We'll grab a bite to eat before we **head for** the airport.
   우린 공항에 가기 전에 식사를 조금 할거야.

2. Chris **is headed to** China for business. 크리스는 출장으로 중국에 가.

A: Let's **head for** the bar, I need a drink! 바에 가자, 술 한잔 해야겠어!

B: I can't, I have a date. 안돼, 나 데이트있어.

start for

> **영영** to serve or substitute for another; to begin to do something
>
> **의미** 1.(운동경기) 선수교체하다   2.뭔가 시작하다

1. A new player will **start for** his injured teammate.
   새로운 선수가 부상당한 동료 대신 뛸거야.

2. I plan to **start for** my PhD this summer.
   난 이번 여름에 박사학위를 시작할 계획이야.

A: I thought you weren't playing soccer.
   난 내가 축구경기에 뛰지 않을거라 생각했는데.

B: I have to **start for** someone who hurt his leg.
   다리를 다친 선수를 대신해 내가 뛰어야 돼.

file for

영영 to make an application for something; to place documents somewhere

의미 1.(이혼, 파산 등) 공식적으로 신청하다   2.고소하다   3.서류를 두다

보충 file a complaint against~하게 되면 문맥에 따라 항의하다 또는 고소하다

1. I have no other choice but to **file for** divorce!
   난 이혼 소송을 낼 수 밖에 없어!

2. There is no doubt about it, he's going to **file for** bankruptcy.
   의심할 여지가 없이 그 사람은 파산신청을 할거야.

A: Ben and Leslie's marriage didn't last long.
   벤과 레슬리의 결혼은 오래가지 못했어.

B: They **filed for** separation shortly after the wedding.
   결혼 직후에 별거를 신청했어.

root for

영영 to cheer on or hope for the success of someone, especially in sports

의미 특히 운동경기에서 응원하다, 지지하다

1. Everyone **roots for** the underdog.   사람들 모두 약체 선수를 응원해.

2. Which World Cup team will you **root for**?
   월드컵 팀 중 어느 팀을 응원할거야?

A: The football championship game is on now.
   미식축구 챔피언 결정전이 지금 하고 있어.

B: I know, and I'm **rooting for** the Eagles.   알아, 난 이글스를 응원해.

Unit 01
Unit 02
Unit 03
Unit 04
Unit 05
Unit 06
Unit 07

go for

영영 to favor; to desire to have something; to be priced or valued at a certain amount; to seek to grab or attack; to travel for something

의미 1.좋아하다 2.해당되다 3.가격이 …로 책정되다 4.공격하다, 달려들다 5.…하러[가지러] 가다

보충 Go for it! 시도하다!, go for a walk 산보하다

1. I never thought you'd **go for** me. 네가 나를 원하는 지 생각 못했어.

2. I was just going to **go for** a walk. You want to come?
   산책하려던 참이었어. 같이 갈래?

A: I'm bored. Shall we **go for** a walk? 따분해. 우리 산책할까?

B: Yes. It will be good exercise. 그래. 운동이 좀 되겠지.

run for

영영 to seek elected office; to move rapidly toward something

의미 1.후보로 나서다   2.…쪽으로 급히 뛰어가다

보충 run for it = make a run for it 도망치다 *run for+시간 …동안 뛰다

1. He plans to **run for** a seat in the Senate.
   걔는 상원의원 자리에 입후보할 계획이야.

2. It started to rain and we **ran for** shelter.
   비가 오기 시작해서 우리는 피신처로 뛰어갔어.

A: Looks like my bus is arriving. 내 버스 도착하는 것 같아.

B: You'd better **run for** it before it leaves. 떠나기 전에 버스 쪽으로 뛰어가.

vote for

영영 to cast a ballot to elect someone

의미 찬성투표하다, 제안하다

1. I think I'd rather **vote for** the other guy.

차라리 다른 사람에게 투표를 하는게 나을 것 같아.

2. I hate them both. I won't **vote for** anyone.

난 둘 다 다 싫어. 누구한테도 투표를 하지 않을거야.

A: This is the most important election in my lifetime.

내 생애 가장 중요한 선거야.

B: You'll have the chance to **vote for** whoever you'd like.

누구든 네가 좋아하는 사람에게 투표할 수 있잖아.

cover for

영영 to assist of help someone by doing their job; to help hide something bad or illegal that someone has done.

의미 1.다른 사람의 일을 대신 처리하다 2.(잘못) 덮어주다

1. I can't work today. Can you **cover for** me?

나 오늘 출근못해. 나 대신 일 좀 처리해줄 수 있어?

2. He **covered for** his boss when the money went missing.

돈의 행방이 묘연해졌을 때 그는 사장의 잘못을 덮어줬어.

A: The FBI couldn't convict him of a crime.

FBI는 그를 범죄로 기소할 수 없었어.

B: He's a crook, and others **are covering for** him.

그는 사기꾼이고 다른 사람들이 그를 보호하고 있어.

trade ~ for

> **영영** exchange something in order to receive another thing, without the use of money
> **의미** 교환하다, 맞바꾸다
> **보충** trade in A for B 'A+돈'을 지급하고 B를 사다

1. You'll have to **trade** your bike **for** a car.
   넌 네 자전거를 차로 바꿔야 할거야

2. She **traded in** her old phone **for** a new one.
   걘 예전 폰에 돈을 더 주고 새로운 폰을 샀어

A: What will happen if you're promoted? 네가 승진하면 어떻게 될까?

B: I'll **trade** this job **for** a better one. 난 더 나은 일자리로 자리를 바꿀거야.

blame ~ for

> **영영** to say someone is responsible for causing a problem
> **의미** 나무라다, 탓하다(blame sb for sth), …의 탓으로 돌리다(blame sth on sb)
> **보충** I don't blame you 그럴만도 해

1. He **blamed** Sam **for** the failure. 걔는 실패를 샘의 탓으로 돌렸어.

2. You shouldn't **blame yourself for** this. 이걸로 널 자책하지마.

A: Cliff is getting a divorce. 클리프가 이혼한대.

B: He **blames** his wife **for** their broken marriage.
   걔는 결혼파탄을 아내탓으로 돌리고 있어.

take ~ for

영영 to believe something about someone or something, which might turn out to be untrue

의미 …을 착각하다, 잘못알다

보충 mistake A for B A를 B로 혼동하다. What do you take me for?(날 뭘로 보는거야?)

1. Do you **take** me **for** a complete idiot? 날 완전 바보로 아는거야?
2. I **took** Pete **for** someone else. 난 피트를 다른 사람으로 착각했어.

A: If you invest with me, you'll become rich. 너 내게 투자하면 부자가 될거야.

B: Don't **take** me **for** a fool. 날 바보로 생각하지마.

think of

영영 to remember or recall; to have a new idea; to have an opinion on something

의미 생각하다, …을 생각해내다

보충 be thinking of[about] ~ing …할 생각이다, …할까 생각중야

1. What do you **think of** the new guy? 새로 입사한 사람 어때?
2. I'm **thinking of** asking her out for a date. 데이트 신청해 볼까 해.

A: Do you ever miss your ex-girlfriend? 네 옛여친 보고 싶은 적 있어?

B: Honestly, I **think of** her all the time. 솔직히 말해서, 계속 걔 생각만 하고 있어.

know of

> **영영** to be aware of something
>
> **의미** …에 대해 알고 있다

1. Do you **know of** any good nightclubs?
어디 좋은 나이트클럽 아는데 있어?

2. I **know of** a guy I could set you up with.
내가 소개시켜줄 수도 있는 남자를 알고 있어.

A: Have you met Bobby Simpkins? 바비 심킨스를 만난 적이 있어?

B: I don't **know of** anyone by that name. 그런 이름의 사람을 알지 못해.

die of

> **영영** to pass away due to a specific cause
>
> **의미** 특정 병으로 죽다
>
> **보충** die of[from] cancer 암으로 죽다

1. He **died of** injuries from the car crash.
걔는 차사고로 입은 부상으로 죽었어.

2. How many people **die from** cancer every year?
매년 암으로 얼마나 많은 사람들이 죽어?

A: The actor's death was unexpected. 그 배우의 죽음은 예상밖이었어.

B: I heard that he **died of** AIDS. 에이즈로 죽었다고 들었어.

Unit 01
Unit 02
Unit 03
Unit 04
Unit 06
Unit 07

hear of

> **영영** to have been given information about something
> **의미** …의 소식을 듣다
> **보충** hear of = hear about

1. I **have** never **heard of** such a thing.
   그런 일이 있다는 것을 들어본 적이 없어.

2. I**'ve heard so much about** you. 당신 얘기 많이 들었어요.

A: Did you **hear about** the office party? 사무실 회식에 관한 얘기들었어?

B: No. What happened? 아니. 어떻게 됐는데?

take care of

> **영영** to protect or nurture a person or thing
> **의미** 1.돌보다(take care of sb)   2.처리하다(take care of sth)

1. I'll **take care of** your daughter while you're out.
   외출할 때 딸을 돌봐줄게.

2. Chris said he'd be willing to **take care of** that.
   크리스가 그것을 기꺼이 처리하겠다고 말했어.

A: I can't find the time to make a dentist appointment.
   치과에 전화 예약할 짬이 안나.

B: Let me **take care of** it for you. You're too busy.
   나한테 맡겨. 넌 너무 바쁘잖아.

Unit 01

Unit 02

Unit 03

Unit 04

Unit 06

Unit 07

make fun of

> **영영** to ridicule or intentionally insult
>
> **의미** 비웃다(joke about; make jokes about)
>
> **보충** make a fool of sb 비웃다, 조롱하다, make a fool of oneself 바보 같은 짓을 하다

1. **Some kids were making fun of** her. 아이들 몇몇이 걔를 놀려댔어.
2. Don't **make fun of** my English accent! 내 영어억양을 비웃지마!

A: I got teased a lot in grade school. 난 초등학교에서 놀림을 많이 받았어.

B: Little kids are cruel and **make fun of** everything.
꼬맹이들은 무자비해서 안 놀리는게 없지.

be sick of

> **영영** to be annoyed or frustrated with a person or situation
>
> **의미** 넌덜머리나다, 지겹다, 질린다
>
> **보충** be sick of = get sick of

1. Don't you **get sick of** that noise? 저 소음에 질리지 않았어?
2. I'm **sick of** hearing you complain all the time.
난 네가 늘상 불평만 늘어놓는데 질렸어.

A: I'm really **getting sick of** spring. 난 정말 여름이 지겨워.

B: I don't like spring all that much myself. 나도 여름이 그렇게 좋지는 않아.

be worthy of

> **영영** to have enough merit to meet a high standard
>
> **의미** …할 가치가 있다(be worth~)

1. Unfortunately, he's **not worthy of** a scholarship.
   불행하게도, 걔는 장학금을 받을 만큼은 아냐.

2. I really don't think Anne **is worthy of** her husband.
   난 앤에게 그녀 남편이 과분하다고 정말 생각해.

A: They didn't allow me to be on the basketball team.
   내가 야구팀에서 뛰는 것을 허락하지 않았어.

B: It takes work to **be worthy of** the team.   팀에서 뛰려면 많은 노력이 필요해.

be aware of

> **영영** to know of, to have information about something
>
> **의미** 알고 있다, 깨닫고 있다
>
> **보충** be aware of 다음에는 명사, that 절, 의문사 절이 올 수 있다.

1. **Are** you **aware of** what your wife is doing?
   네 아내가 뭘 하고 있는지 알고 있어?

2. I'm **well aware of** that. But there's nothing I can do.
   그거 잘 알고 있어. 하지만 내가 할 수 있는 게 아무 것도 없어.

A: Were you invited to join the science club?
   과학클럽에 들어오라는 초대를 받았어?

B: Sure. I'm **aware of** where they will meet.
   그래. 걔네들이 어디서 만날지 알고 있어.

be proud of

> **영영** to feel a sense of pleasure or satisfaction about personal qualities or achievements
>
> **의미** …을 자랑스러워하다
>
> **보충** be proud of = take pride in = pride oneself on

1. I'm **so proud of** your recent promotion.
   네가 최근 승진한게 자랑스러워.

2. I bet your mom **is really proud of** you.
   네 엄마가 너를 자랑스럽게 생각하겠구나.

A: I got the highest score in the class! 내가 우리 반에서 제일 좋은 점수를 받았어!

B: Way to go! I'm **so proud of** you. 잘했구나! 네가 정말 자랑스러워.

rob ~ of

> **영영** to steal or take illegally; to take away in a cruel manner
>
> **의미** 훔치다
>
> **보충** rob+사람/은행/가게+of~, steal sth from+사람/은행/가게

1. Thieves **robbed** Carol **of** all her jewelry.
   도둑들이 캐롤의 보석류를 다 훔쳤어.

2. Who would **steal** shoes **from** a party? 누가 파티에서 신발을 훔치겠어?

A: Thieves got into your hotel room in Rome?
   도둑들이 로마 네 호텔방에 들어왔다고?

B: We **were robbed of** most of our money. 우린 가진 돈 거의 다 도둑맞았어.

Unit 01
Unit 02
Unit 03
Unit 04
Unit 05
Unit 07

accuse A of B

> **영영** to publicly say that someone did something wrong or bad
> **의미** 비난하다, 고소하다
> **보충** accuse sb of sth[~ing]

1. My wife **accused** me **of** cheating on her.
내 아내는 자기 몰래 바람폈다고 비난했어.

2. Don't **accuse** me **of** being dishonest! 내가 부정직하다고 비난하지마!

A: I think Chris stole my wallet. 크리스가 내 지갑을 훔쳐간 것 같아.

B: It's not good to **accuse** people **of** things. 사람들을 의심하는 것은 좋지 않아.

inform A of B

> **영영** to pass along information about something
> **의미** …에게 …에 관한 정보를 주다
> **보충** of 대신에 about을 써서 inform A about B라 해도 된다.

1. The university **informed** him **of** his acceptance.
그 대학교는 걔에게 합격통지를 했어.

2. **Inform** us **of** changes in the situation. 상황변화에 대해 우리에게 알려줘.

A: I'm sorry, but Mrs. Paulson just died.
유감입니다만, 폴슨 부인께서는 방금 돌아가셨어요.

B: I'd better **inform** her husband **of** her death.
남편께 사망소식을 알려야겠네요.

Unit 01

Unit 02

Unit 03

Unit 04

Unit 06

Unit 07

run short of

> 영영 to not have enough, to use the last of something
>
> 의미 다 써서 부족하다, 모자라다
>
> 보충 run short of = run low of = be out of = be short of

1. Sorry, we're **running short of** beer. 미안하지만, 맥주가 부족해.

2. Come on! Hurry! We're **running out of** time!
   어서! 서둘러! 시간이 없다고!

A: I'm afraid of **running out of** money. 돈이 바닥날까봐 걱정돼.

B: So get a better job. 그럼 더 나은 직장을 가져.

fall short of

> 영영 to not be able to complete something, especially related
> to competing with others or accomplishing a goal
>
> 의미 기대치에 이르지 못하다, 달성못하다
>
> 보충 fall short of ~ing …까지는 하지 않다

1. I **fell short of** losing 15 pounds. 난 15파운드를 빼지 못했어.

2. The runner **fell short of** the Olympic record.
   그 주자는 올림픽 기록에 못미쳤어.

A: Why are you always exercising? 왜 항상 운동을 하는거야?

B: I don't want to **fall short of** my fitness goal.
   목표로 하는 몸매에 달성못하는게 싫어서.

remind ~ of

영영 to ask someone to recall something; to be reminded of something because of experiencing something similar

의미 주어를 보니 …가 …을 기억나게 하다

보충 That reminds me of~ 그걸 보니 …가 생각나

1. You can **remind** him **of** his promise.
   너는 걔한테 걔가 한 약속을 기억하게 해.

2. **Remind** me **about** the doctor's appointment.
   병원예약한 거 내가 기억나게 해줘.

A: You seem to like Ken. 넌 켄을 좋아하는 것 같아.

B: He **reminds** me **of** my brother. 걜보면 내 오빠가 생각나.

make a mess of

영영 to cause disorder or problems; to do poor or incompetent work

의미 엉망으로 만들다, 망치다

1. Sam tried to help, he **made a mess of** it.
   샘은 도와줄려고 했지만 일을 망쳤어.

2. I'm so sorry that I **made a mess of** everything.
   다 엉망으로 만들어 미안해.

A: Weren't you going to write a novel? 소설을 쓰는거 아녔어?

B: I tried, but I **made a mess of** it. 시도했는데 엉망이 됐어.

put on

영영 to trick or fool; to stage a performance; to dress in clothing or apply make up

의미 1.속이다　2.무대에 올리다　3.옷을 입다　4.화장을 하다　5.음악을 틀다

보충 put on too much make-up 화장을 너무 많이 하다, put some much on 음악을 좀 틀다

1. You got to **put on** some lipstick. 넌 립스틱을 좀 발라야 돼.

2. What would you like me to **put on** your hotdog?
핫도그에 뭘 발라드릴까요?

A: I **put on** too much make-up. I look like a clown.
화장을 너무 많이 했나봐. 광대처럼 보여.

B: No, you don't. But I would remove that eyeliner.
아니야. 그렇지 않아. 정 그러면 내가 눈썹 화장을 지워줄게.

get on

영영 to sit or stand atop of something; to board something like a train, bus or airplane; to do well

의미 1.올라타다　2.기차, 버스, 비행기 등을 타다　3.잘하다, 잘 지내다

보충 get on은 타는 이동수단이 높은 경우이고 낮은 택시 등을 타다라고 할 때는 get in, 인터넷에 접속하다는 get on the Internet

1. You'd better **get on** the train. It's leaving. 열차에 타. 떠난다.

2. How **are** your parents **getting on**? 부모님은 어떻게 지내셔?

A: You didn't catch the train to your hometown? 고향행 기차를 타지 못했어?

B: There wasn't enough time to **get on.** 탈 시간이 충분하지 않았어.

plan on

영영 to anticipate something happening in the future; to indicate an intention to do something

의미 1.기대하다 2.…할 생각이다

보충 plan to+V = plan on ~ing

1. We slept together. I didn't **plan on** it. I didn't mean to.
우리는 함께 잤어. 계획에 없던거야. 그럴 생각이 아니었어.

2. How do you **plan on** getting out of here?
여기서 어떻게 빠져나갈 생각이야?

A: What're you **planning to** do at the end of the day?
일과 후에 뭐할 생각이야?

B: I **was planning on** resting but I might change my mind.
쉴 생각이었지만 바뀔 수도 있고.

wait on

영영 to bring food in a restaurant; to stay until a certain time or until someone arrives

의미 1.식당 등에서 시중들다(wait on sb) 2.…을 기다리다

1. The restaurant staff will **wait on** us. 식당 직원들이 우리를 서빙할거야.

2. I'm **waiting on** one of my friends. 난 내 친구들중 한 명을 기다리고 있어.

A: I don't see anyone at this bistro. 이 작은 식당엔 아무도 없네.

B: See if you can call someone to **wait on** us.
시중들 사람 부를 수 있는지 알아봐.

try on

> **영영** to put on clothing, usually in a store, to see if it feels good and to see if the person would like to buy it
>
> **의미** 주로 가게에서 옷이나 구두가 맞는지, 맘에 드는지 한번 입어보다.(try it on)
>
> **보충** 한번 먹어보다는 try+음식명사

1. You'd better **try on** that shirt to see if it fits.
   그 셔츠가 맞는지 한번 입어봐.

2. I don't have time to **try on** new clothes. 새 옷을 입어볼 시간이 없어.

A: These shoes are too tight on my feet. 이 신발은 발에 너무 꽉 끼여.

B: Didn't you **try** them **on** before you bought them?
   사기 전에 신어보지 않았어?

carry on

> **영영** to be unpleasantly loud; to continue doing something; to bring an object
>
> **의미** 1.투덜대다 2.계속하다 3.…을 가져오다[지니다]
>
> **보충** 계속하다라고 할 때는 특히 carry on with sth 혹은 carry on ~ing라 한다.

1. Are you going to **carry on with** your meeting?
   너 회의를 계속할거야?

2. Just forget it and **carry on with** what you're doing.
   그냥 잊어버리고 하던 일이나 계속해라.

A: You've got to **carry on with** the report. 넌 이 보고서를 계속 작성해야 돼.

B: It will be finished in a few hours. 몇 시간 내로 끝날거야.

cheat on

영영 to do something that illegal or unfair, especially on an exam; to have sex with a person while in a relationship with another person

의미 1.부정행위를 하다   2.몰래 바람피다(cheat on sb with~)

1. I hear you're cheating on me with an analyst.
네가 날 속이고 애널리스트와 바람핀다고 하던대.

2. It's not okay to cheat people out of money.
사람들 사기쳐서 돈을 뺏는 것은 안돼.

A: Would you ever cheat on your girlfriend?   여친 몰래 바람핀 적 있어?

B: Never! I love her too much to do that to her.
전혀! 걔한테 그렇게 하기에는 너무 사랑해.

fall on

영영 to drop to the ground; to be responsible for; to experience difficult times

의미 1.…에 넘어지다   2.책임을 지다   3.어려운 시기를 겪다   4.(생일, 기념일이) 언제 …이다

1. I can't believe you laughed when I fell on the ice.
내가 얼음 위에 넘어졌을 때 네가 어떻게 웃을 수가 있어.

2. My birthday will fall on a Sunday this year.
내 생일은 금년에 일요일이야.

A: This is a very heavy sculpture.   이건 아주 무거운 조각인데.

B: It hurt a lot when it fell on my foot.   내 발에 떨어졌을 때 엄청 아팠어.

come on

> **영영** to seek the attention of a possible sexual partner
> **의미** 상대방이 원치 않는데 성적으로 들이대다, 유혹하다(come on to sb)
> **보충** give sb the come-on 수작걸다

1. He **came on to** us after drinking too much.
   걘 과음을 한 후에 우리에게 수작을 걸었어.

2. I can't stand how guys **come on to** me when I go out.
   내가 외출할 때 남자들이 어찌나 내게 추근대는지 참을 수가 없어.

A: Did Chris **come on to** you at all? 크리스가 네게 수작을 걸었어?

B: No, he acted like a perfect gentleman. 아니, 걘 완전 신사처럼 행동했어.

count on

> **영영** to depend on or trust
> **의미** 의지하다, 기대하다, 믿다(count on sb [for~/to+V/~ing])
> **보충** count on = depend on = rely on = rest on = hinge on

1. I **count on** you to help me out. 난 네가 날 도와줄거라 믿어.

2. You can't **count on** anyone to be honest.
   넌 아무나 정직하다고 믿어서는 안돼.

A: Please get it done right away. 지금 당장 이것 좀 해줘.

B: Don't worry, you can **count on** me. 걱정마. 나만 믿어.

work on

영영 to attempt to improve or complete; to try to influence someone

의미 1.주의를 기울여 끝내지 못한 일을 하다 2.영향을 주다, 설득하다(work on sb)

보충 work on+시간명사는 work on에 해당되지 않는다. 그냥 …에 일하다.

1. Do you have to **work on** a big project? 중요한 일을 해야 되는거야?

2. I'll **work on** her to get it done. 빨리 끝내라고 설득할게.

A: I'm going to **work on** this stuff at home tonight.
오늘 밤 집에서 이 일을 할거야.

B: If you have any problems give me a call. 문제가 생기면 나한테 전화해.

go on

영영 to continue; to get on board or into something

의미 1.계속하다(go on with~) 2.일어나다

보충 go on sth…을 시작하다, go on strike 파업하다, go on a walk 산책하다, go on a trip 여행하다

1. Just **go on with** the work you were doing. 네가 하고 있던 일을 계속해.

2. I can't **go on with** this relationship. 난 이 관계를 계속할 수가 없어.

A: Are you planning to quit? 너 그만 둘 생각이야?

B: No, I'll **go on** working here. 아니, 여기서 계속 일할거야.

insist on

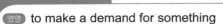

> 영영 to make a demand for something
>
> 의미 1.주장하다, 요구하다   2.…을 고집하다
>
> 보충 insist on sth; insist on ~ing

1. Some people **insist on** a window seat in restaurants.
   식당에서 창가좌석을 고집하는 사람들도 있어.

2. She **insists on** exercising every morning.
   걘 매일 아침 운동을 계속하고 있어.

A: Why did you let Molly come with you? 넌 왜 몰리를 데려온거야?

B: She **insisted on** having breakfast with us.
   걔가 우리와 함께 아침을 먹겠다고 고집폈어.

turn on

> 영영 to switch on power for something; to become sexually aroused
>
> 의미 1.스위치를 돌려서 켜다   2.성적으로 흥분되다(↔ turn off)
>
> 보충 turn(-)on 흥분, 흥분시키는 사람

1. I'm not sure how to **turn on** this cell phone.
   이 핸드폰을 어떻게 켜야 하는지 모르겠어.

2. You're sexy, you **turn** me **on**. 넌 섹시해. 넌 날 꼴리게 해.

A: Can you find that information for me? 그 정보 좀 찾아줄래?

B: Hold on a second. I need to **turn on** my computer. 잠깐. 컴퓨터 좀 켜고.

check on

> **영영** to verify or monitor something; to look into something to see if it is true or accurate
>
> **의미** 뭐가 제대로 되었는지 안전은 한지 등을 조회하다, 확인하다

1. I called my apartment and **checked on** my grandpa.
   할아버지가 괜찮으신지 아파트에 전화했어.

2. I **checked on** her but she's a little unstable today.
   걜 확인해봤더니 오늘 좀 불안정한 상태야.

A: Is the office manager around? 실장있어?

B: She went to **check on** some reports. 보고서 확인하러 갔습니다.

hold on

> **영영** to grip tightly; to wait; to endure during a difficult situation
>
> **의미** 1.꽉잡다(hold on to) 2.기다리다 3.어려운 시기를 견디다
>
> **보충** hold on to~는 뭔가 떨어트리지 않기 위해 혹은 넘어지지 않기 위해 …을 손으로 꽉 잡고 있다, 집착하다

1. Can you **hold on** a moment? I have another call.
   잠시만 기다려 줄래? 다른 전화가 왔어.

2. **Hold on**, let me go get Chris. 잠깐만, 내가 가서 크리스를 데려올게.

A: There's a telephone call for Bill. 빌에게 전화왔는데.

B: **Hold on**, I'll go find him. 잠깐, 내가 가서 찾아볼게.

hit on

영영 to attempt to interest someone in sexual interaction

의미 1.불현듯 생각해내다(hit on sth) 2.수작걸다(hit on sb)

1. I have **hit on** a solution to this problem.
난 이 문제에 대한 해결책을 생각해냈어.

2. **Are** you **hitting on** me? 너 나한테 수작거는거야?

A: How was the discovery made? 그 발견은 어떻게 된거야?

B: Scientists **hit on** it in their lab. 과학자들이 실험실에서 생각해낸거래.

grow on

영영 to become more favorable or familiar; to support life in a certain place

의미 주어가 on 이하의 사람에게 자라다, 커나가다, 맘을 사로잡다, sb가 주어를 좋아지게 되다

보충 주어자리에는 sb도 올 수 있다. 예문 2번 참고.

1. This Thai food **is** really **growing on** me.
이 태국음식은 정말 좋아지고 있어.

2. I hated George but he's **grown on** me.
난 조지를 싫어했는데 점점 좋아졌어.

A: I see you eat a lot of kimchi. 네가 김치를 많이 먹는 걸 봤어.

B: The taste of it **grew on** me after a while.
조금 시간이 지난 후에 그 맛이 점점 좋아졌어.

take on

- **영영** to shoulder a burden; to oppose someone or something
- **의미** 1. 책임지다, 떠맡다   2. 신규채용하다   3. 맞서다, 대항하다
- **보충** take on sth …에 대한 의견. What's your take on~? …에 대한 네 의견은 어때?

1. We need to **take on** another employee in the warehouse.
   창고에 직원을 한명 더 고용해야겠어.

2. You can't **take on** the boss and win. 넌 사장에게 맞서서 이길 수 없어.

A: How did Brad get beat up? 브래드는 어떡하다 얻어 터진거야?

B: He **took on** someone tougher than him. 갠 자기보다 터프한 사람에게 맞섰어.

stand on

- **영영** to be in an upright position, on one's feet
- **의미** …에 대한 특정한 입장이나 의견을 가지고 있다
- **보충** from where I stand 내 생각으로는, stand on one's two feet 독립하다, 자립하다

1. I don't know where the candidate **stands on** taxes.
   난 그 후보자가 세금에 어떤 입장인지 몰라.

2. I'm trying my hardest to **stand on** my own two feet.
   자립하기 위해서 최선을 다하는 중이야.

A: My new girlfriend is very religious. 내 새 여친은 매우 독실해.

B: How does she **stand on** premarital sex? 혼전 섹스에 대해서는 어떻게 생각해?

be on

> **영영** to be powered up; to be responsible for something
>
> **의미** 1. 전원이 켜져 있다   2. …을 책임지다

1. Don't touch the TV, it's **on** already. TV 손대지마, 켜져 있어.
2. It **is on** you to keep things calm. 상황을 진정시키는건 네 책임이야.

A: Has anyone told Sam that his father died?
누가 샘에게 아버지 돌아가셨다는 말을 했어?

B: It **is on** me to deliver the bad news. 나쁜 소식을 전하는건 내 몫이야.

catch on

> **영영** to start to understand, to learn how to do something; to become a trend
>
> **의미** 1. 이해가 빠르다   2. 유행하다

1. Excellent idea! You're **catching on**. 좋은 생각이야! 머리 잘 돌아가네.
2. How do things like that **catch on**? 그런 것이 어떻게 유행을 할까?

A: That is the ugliest sweater I've seen. 이런 추한 스웨터는 처음본다.

B: The trend for those sweaters **has caught on**.
그런 스웨터 추세가 유행이야.

focus on

> **영영** to pay close attention to one person or thing
> **의미** 집중하다

1. **The report will focus on increasing profit.**
   그 보고서는 수익증가에 집중할거야.

2. **I plan to focus on getting promoted.** 난 승진하는데 집중할 생각이야.

A: **What are you going to focus on in school?** 학교에서 뭐에 집중할거야?

B: **I want to get a medical degree.** 의사학위를 받고 싶어.

move on

> **영영** to do other things; to go to another location; to get over a traumatic or sad situation
> **의미** 1.다음 일을 하다 2.다른 장소로 가다 3.어려운 상황을 이겨내다, 극복하다
> **보충** get a move on 서두르다, make a move on 추근대다

1. **I failed at this job, so I'm going to move on.**
   난 이 일에 실패했어. 다른 일로 넘어갈거야.

2. **You need to move on after your divorce.** 넌 이혼을 잘 극복해야 돼.

A: **I was so in love with Chris.** 난 크리스를 너무 사랑했었어.

B: **It's time to move on and find a new man.**
   이젠 극복하고 새로운 사람을 찾아야지.

pick on

> **영영** to single someone out for ridicule or bad treatment
> **의미** 괴롭히다, 못살게 굴다
> **보충** = find fault with

1. Stop **picking on** me. 날 못살게 굴지 마, 놀리지 마.
2. Why do you always **pick on** me? 왜 늘상 나를 놀리는거야?

A: My son is so unhappy at his school. 내 아들은 학교에서 즐겁지 못해.

B: Is anyone **picking on** him there? 학교에서 누가 괴롭히는거야?

click on

> **영영** to turn on the power; to open something on a computer using a mouse
> **의미** 전원을 켜다, 마우스를 이용해 열다

1. **Click on** that icon to open the file. 아이콘을 클릭해서 파일을 열어봐.
2. **Click on** the a/c remote because it's getting hot.
   더우니까 에어컨 리모콘을 눌러봐.

A: My computer was shut down by a virus.
   내 컴퓨터가 바이러스에 감염돼 고장났어.

B: Did you **click on** any unknown files? 확인되지 않은 파일을 뭐 클릭한거야?

Unit 01
Unit 02
Unit 03
Unit 04
Unit 06
Unit 07

pin ~on

> **영영** to falsely accuse or convict someone of something bad; to affix something, usually to clothing
>
> **의미** 1. 잘못에 대해 …에게 책임을 씌우다 2. 옷 등에 …을 고정시키다
>
> **보충** pin the blame on sb sb에게 책임을 지우다

1. Don't try to **pin** these problems **on** me.
   이 문제들이 내 책임인 것처럼 만들려고 하지마.

2. My boss **pins the blame on** other employees.
   우리 사장은 다른 직원들에게 책임을 돌리려고 해.

A: The police tried to **pin** the drugs **on** me.
경찰이 내가 약물을 복용했다고 뒤집어 씌울려고 했어.

B: But you've never used drugs in your life. 하지만 넌 평생 약을 한 적이 없잖아.

be hard on

> **영영** to be harsh or unkind to someone, to treat badly
>
> **의미** 모질게 대하다, 못되게 굴다
>
> **보충** ↔ go easy on, be hard on oneself 자책하다

1. I think it will **be very hard on** your kids.
   그게 아이들을 힘들게 할 것 같아.

2. Please try not to **be hard on** him, it's his first real job.
   걔 너무 힘들게 하지마, 실제 직장일은 처음이야.

A: Do you have to **be so hard on** Jeff? 넌 제프에게 그렇게 모질게 대해야 돼?

B: I'm afraid he will make another big mistake.
개가 또 큰 실수를 할까 봐서 그래.

log on to

> **영영** to officially enter a computer site
> **의미** 인터넷에 접속하다
> **보충** = get online = get connected to the Internet

1. You can **log on to** the Internet with this password.
   이 패스워드로 인터넷에 접속할 수 있어.

2. I don't have time to **log on to** the site today.
   난 오늘 이 사이트에 접속할 시간이 없어.

A: It's amazing how much information is on the web.
   웹상에 있는 많은 정보가 정말 놀라워.

B: Billions of people **log on to** the Internet daily.
   수많은 사람들이 매일 인터넷에 접속해.

sneak on

> **영영** to secretly get into or on top of something
> **의미** 1.선생님이나 부모님에게 일러바치다(sneak on sb)　　2.몰래 다가가다
> (sneak up on sb)

1. They **snuck up on** me and scared me.
   걔네들이 내게 몰래 다가와 나를 놀라게 했어.

2. You'll have to **sneak on** the bus with me.
   넌 나와 함께 몰래 버스에 올라타야 될거야.

A: I thought the train seats had been sold out.
   열차 좌석이 매진인 걸로 생각했는데.

B: Yeah, but I **snuck on** it so I could get here.
   맞아, 하지만 몰래 타고서 여기에 왔지.

pass on

영영 to die; to give to someone else, to decline or say no

의미 1.죽다 2.건네주다 3.거절하다

1. My grandmother **passed on** when she was 93.
   할머니는 93세에 돌아가셨어.

2. We decided to **pass on** the items to other people.
   우리는 물품들을 다른 사람들에게 나눠주기로 했어.

A: Did your uncle die recently? 최근에 삼촌이 돌아가셨어?

B: Yes. He **passed on** when he was fairly young.
   어. 꽤 젊으신데 돌아가셨어.

to·with·about

to
…로, 대상, 접촉, 비교, 소속
ex. owe to, belong to

with
…와 함께, …을(대상)
ex. go with, mess with

about
…에 관하여, …의 주위에
ex. think about, get about

have to

> **영영** to be obligated, to need to do something, especially as a duty
>
> **의미** …을 해야 한다, should, ought to보다 의무의 무게가 무겁다.
>
> **보충** have to = have got to

1. I **have to** cancel tomorrow's meeting. 내일 회의를 취소해야 돼.

2. I **had to** stay until everything was finished.
   난 다 끝날 때까지 남아있어야 했었어.

A: You **have to** stay late tonight. 넌 오늘 밤 야근해야 돼.

B: You can't be serious. I want to go home. 이럴 수가. 나 집에 가고 싶어.

like to

> **영영** to enjoy something; to express a wish to do something
>
> **의미** 일반적으로 …을 좋아하거나, …하는 것을 좋아한다
>
> **보충** like to+V = like ~ing

1. I don't **like** doing the washing. 설거지하는 것을 싫어해.

2. Does she **like to** eat seafood? 걔 해산물 먹는 것 좋아해?

A: Do you **like to** buy Apple products? 애플 제품을 사는 걸 좋아해?

B: Sure, they are as good as any other products.
   그럼, 다른 어떤 제품보다 처지지 않잖아.

would like to

> **영영** to express a hope to do something in the future
>
> **의미** 지금 당장 갖고 싶거나 하고 싶은 것을 나타낼 때 사용하는 표현. …하고 싶어.
>
> **보충** want to+V …하고 싶어

1. **Would** you **like to** go out to lunch with me? 나랑 점심 먹으러 나갈래?
2. I **would like** you **to** come to my party. 네가 내 파티에 오기를 바래.

A: This is Pizza Hut. Can I help you? 피자헛입니다. 도와드릴까요?

B: Yes, I'**d like to** order a large pizza. 네. 피자 라지 한 판 주문하고 싶은데요.

come to

> **영영** to arrive at; to reach a total; to wake up from being made unconscious
>
> **의미** 1.…에 도착하다 2.총합이 …되다 3.의식을 찾다
>
> **보충** come to+장소 …에 오다. come to+V …하러 오다. come back to~ 다시 오다

1. He didn't **come back to** my room last night.
   걔가 지난밤에 내 방에 돌아오지 않았어.
2. She **came back to** help me. 걔가 나를 도와주러 왔어.

A: Is Fred in the office now? 프레드 지금 사무실에 있어?

B: Yeah, he **came back to** get his glasses. 어. 안경가지러 다시 돌아왔어.

get to

영영 to start work on something; to annoy or affect someone; to arrive

의미 1.뭔가 일을 시작하다 2.화나게 하다 3.도착하다(get to+장소)

보충 get to know sb 시간을 두고 천천히 알아가다

1. You really want to **get to** know me? 넌 정말 나랑 친해지고 싶어?
2. I would like to **get to** know you. 난 너하고 친해지고 싶어.

A: I'd like to **get to** know the new girl. 새로운 여자애와 친해지고 싶어.

B: Come over here and I'll introduce you. 이리와, 내가 소개시켜줄게.

go to (college)

영영 to begin or continue attending a school

의미 대학에 가다, 대학에 진학하다

보충 went to college 대학에 진학했어, went to[got into] Harvard 하버드에 들어갔다

1. Tom **went to college** in California. 탐은 캘리포니아에 있는 대학에 다녔어.
2. Don't you know Tony **went to** Harvard for an MBA?
   토니가 MBA 따러 하버드에 간 것을 몰랐어?

A: What will Aurora do after high school? 오로라는 고등학교 졸업후 뭐할거야?

B: I think she'll **go to college.** 대학에 진학하겠지.

Unit 01

Unit 02

Unit 03

Unit 04

Unit 05

Unit 06

Unit 07

plan to

영영 to intend to do something in the future; to arrange something with future intent

의미 ···할 계획이다, ···할 생각이다

보충 be planning to+V ···할 생각이다

1. I'm **planning to** go to a movie this evening.
오늘 저녁에 영화보러 갈 생각이야.

2. Yesterday my boss asked me if I **planned to** change jobs!
또한 어제 우리 사장이 나더러 직장을 옮길 생각이냐고 묻더라!

A: I'm **planning to** buy a new car. 새 차를 사려고 해.

B: What kind are you thinking of? 어떤 종류를 생각하고 있는데?

try to

영영 to attempt to do something

의미 해보다, 시도하다

보충 try+명사, try to+V, try+~ing

1. I'm going to **try** starting up my own business.
난 사업을 시작해볼까 해.

2. I'm **trying to** figure out if Jane likes me or not.
제인이 날 좋아하는지 안좋아하는지 알아보고 있어.

A: What happened with Chris last night? 지난 밤에 크리스와 어떻게 됐어?

B: I **tried to** kiss him, but failed. 키스를 하려고 했는데 실패했어.

fail to

영영 to have been unable to do something, to have been unsuccessful

의미 1.실패하다, …하지 못하다, …을 해내지 못하다   2.(사물주어) 고장나다, 작동이 안되다

보충 never fail to+V 반드시 …하다, fail to see[understand] …가 이해가 안돼

1. He **failed to** show up for our date. 걘 우리 데이트하는데 나타나지 않았어.
2. The car **failed to** stop at the traffic light. 그 차는 신호등에 서지를 못했어.

A: Were the people rescued from the house fire?
   그 불난 집에서 사람들은 구조됐어?

B: No, the firemen **failed to** get to them. 아니, 소방관들이 구하지 못했어.

happen to

영영 to have been by chance, to experience something that wasn't planned

의미 1.…에게 일어나다(happen to sb)   2.우연히 …하다, 마침 …하다 (happen to+V)

1. I hope that doesn't **happen to** us! 우리에게는 그런 일이 안 생겼으면 해!
2. Do you **happen to** know where I put my glasses?
   혹시 내가 안경을 어디에 두었는지 알아?

A: Can you recommend a good therapist to me?
   좋은 심리 치료사 좀 추천해 주실 수 있으세요?

B: Yes, I **happen to** know a very good psychiatrist.
   예, 마침 아주 훌륭한 정신과 의사를 알고 있어요.

listen to

영영 to carefully take in information that is being spoken; to hear, as in the case of music

의미 듣다, 귀기울이다

보충 listen to sb+V ···가 ···하는 것을 듣다

1. I would **listen to** music when I rode the subway.
   난 전철을 탈 때는 음악을 듣곤 했어.

2. You just don't **listen to** me anymore. 넌 더 이상 내 말을 안들어.

A: I'm sorry, but let me explain why I did it.
   미안해, 하지만 내가 왜 그랬는지 설명할게

B: I really don't have time to **listen to** you now.
   지금은 네 얘기를 들을 시간이 정말 없다니까.

mean to

영영 to intend to do something; to be unkind or cruel

의미 1.···하려고 하다, ···할 생각이다 2.야비한(be mean to sb)

보충 I don't mean to do ~ (사과하면서)···할 생각은 없어, I didn't mean to + V···하려고 한 건 아니었어

1. I didn't **mean to** interrupt, but you have an important phone call. 방해할 생각은 없지만, 중요한 전화가 왔어.

2. Don't **be so mean to** your wife. 네 부인에게 야비하게 굴지마.

A: How could you do this to me. 어떻게 내게 그럴 수 있어?

B: I really didn't **mean to** make you miserable. 널 비참하게 할려고 한 건 아냐.

ask ~ to

> **영영** to make a request of someone
> **의미** …에게 …해달라고 부탁하다, 요청하다
> **보충** 친구나 아랫사람에게는 tell sb to+V를 쓴다.

1. I'm going to **ask** Susan **to** go on a trip with me.
수잔에게 나와 함께 여행가자고 말해볼거야.

2. Why don't you **ask** her **to** join us? 쟤도 함께 하자고 물어보자.

A: Did you **ask** her **to** marry you? 걔한테 결혼하자고 했어?

B: I couldn't. I was too nervous. 그렇게 할 수가 없었어. 너무 긴장해서 말야.

take ~ to

> **영영** to escort or transport
> **의미** …을 …로 데리고 가다(take sb (out) to+장소) = take sb out for+음식
> **보충** take sb to lunch …을 데리고 가 점심을 사주다, take sb to the hospital …을 병원에 데려가다

1. I'm available to **take** her **to** the airport.
난 걔를 공항에 데려다 줄 시간이 돼.

2. I'll **take** you **out** for a beer to celebrate after work.
내가 일 끝나고 축하하는 의미로 맥주 한잔 살게.

A: Could I possibly ask you to **take** this **to** the front desk?
이것을 프론트데스크로 가져다 줄래?

B: I can take it when I leave for a smoke. 담배 피우러 나갈 때 가져갈게.

learn to

영영 to be taught how to do something; to gain an ability through experience

의미 …하는 것을 배우다, 경험을 통해서 습득하다

보충 learn how to+V(…하는 법을 배우다) ↔ teach sb how to+V(…하는 법을 가르쳐주다)

1. Where did you **learn to** speak English? 어디서 영어회화를 배웠어?
2. You have to **learn how to** do things on your own.
   넌 <u>스스로</u> 해나가는 법을 익혀야 해.

A: Where did you **learn to** do that? 그거 하는 법을 어디서 배운거야?

B: My mom taught me how to do it. 엄마가 그 방법을 알려주셨어.

belong to

영영 to be a member of a group; to be owned by someone

의미 …의 것이다, …에 속하다

보충 belong to sb …의 것이다, belong to sth …의 소속이다, belongings 소지품

1. It must **belong to** the previous owner. 그건 틀림없이 전 주인 것일거야.
2. Does he **belong to** your club? 걔 너희 클럽소속이야?

A: Who left their shoes on my floor? 누가 내 바닥에 신발을 벗어놓고 간거야?

B: I think they **belong to** Jennifer. 제니퍼일거야.

decide to

> **영영** to choose to do something, to affirm something will be done
>
> **의미** ···하기로 결정하다, ···하기로 마음먹다 ☞ 과거 혹은 현재완료형(I've decided to+V)이 많이 쓰인다.

1. I've decided to break up with her. 재랑 헤어지기로 결정했어.
2. Mindy decided to give him another chance.
   민디는 걔한테 한 번 더 기회를 주기로 했어.

A: I've decided to take a holiday and go to Paris!
   휴가받아서 파리에 가기로 했어!
B: Wild! I wish I was going! 근사한데! 나도 갔음 좋겠다!

lie to

> **영영** to be intentionally dishonest or untruthful
>
> **의미** ···에게 거짓말하다(tell a lie)
>
> **보충** lie to sb (about sth) ···에게 (···에 대해) 거짓말을 하다

1. You'd better not lie to your mom. 네 엄마에게 거짓말하지마.
2. I will be in trouble. I told a lie to my boss.
   난 곤란해질거야. 사장에게 거짓말했거든.

A: Why did you lie to me about working here?
   왜 여기서 일하는 걸 내게 거짓말한거야?
B: Because I was ashamed. 쪽 팔려서.

move to

영영 to change residences; to shift from one area to another

의미 이사하다, 이동하다

보충 move out 이사나가다

1. Don't **move to** another city. 다른 도시로 이사가지마.
2. I've decided to **move to** Japan this year.
   올해 일본으로 이사가기로 했어.

A: Do you still have that old motorbike? 너 그 낡은 오토바이 아직 갖고 있어?

B: No, I left it behind when I **moved to** New York.
아니, 뉴욕으로 이사갈 때 버렸어.

deserve to

영영 to merit a reward, often because of ability or good behavior

의미 …할 자격이 있다

보충 You deserve it(넌 그럴 자격이 있어), You deserve more than that(너는 그 이상 받을 자격이 돼)

1. You **deserved to** ace it. Congrats. 넌 시험에서 A를 받을 만해. 축하해.
2. I get that you're mad. You **deserve to** be mad.
   너 화난 것을 이해해. 너는 화가 날 만하지.

A: You **deserve to** get the highest award. 넌 최우수상을 받을 자격이 있어.

B: I was just doing my job, sir. 전 그냥 제 일을 한 것뿐인데요.

used to

> 영영 to have done something in the past, but not do it in the present
>
> 의미 현재는 그렇지 않지만 과거에 …하곤 했었다
>
> 보충 be[get] used to+명사[~ing] …하는데 적응하다, be used to+동사 …하는데 사용되다

1. Sam **used to** live in LA. Now she lives in Chicago.
   샘은 과거에 LA에 살았지만 지금은 시카고에 살아.

2. There **used to** be a big tree in the park. 공원에 큰 나무가 있었어.

A: Does Tim know Jennifer very well? 팀은 제니퍼하고 아주 친해?

B: Sure. They **used to** work together. 그럼. 두 사람은 예전에 함께 일했었는걸.

get used to

> 영영 to become accustomed to or familiar with
>
> 의미 …에 익숙하다, 적응하다
>
> 보충 get[be] accustomed to+명사[~ing]

1. You'll **get used to** this place. 넌 이 곳에 익숙해질거야.

2. I guess it'll take while to **get used to** this.
   이거 적응하는데 어느 정도 시간이 걸릴 것 같아.

A: How do you like your new apartment? 새 아파트 어때?

B: It took a while to **get used to** it. 익숙해지는데 좀 시간이 필요했어.

choose to

> **영영** to decide to do something out of numerous choices
> **의미** …하기로 선택하다, 결정하다
> **보충** choose not to+V …하지 않기로 결정하다

1. You **chose to** travel to Hollywood? 할리우드에 여행하기로 했다며?
2. I **chose to** become a teacher years ago. 오래 전에 선생님이 되기로 했어.

A: Why did you **choose to** get married to your wife?
  너는 왜 네 아내와 결혼하기로 했니?

B: To me, she seemed better than anyone else.
  나한테 있어서, 내 아내는 그 누구보다도 좋은 사람인 것 같았거든.

apologize to

> **영영** to express regret for something, often by admitting a fault
> **의미** …에게 사과하다
> **보충** apologize to sb for sth …에게 …일을 사과하다

1. I came to **apologize to** you. 네게 사과하러 왔어.
2. I really think that you should **apologize to** Julie.
  내 생각에 넌 줄리에게 사과해야 돼.

A: Chris was very offended by your actions.
  크리스는 네 행동에 무척 기분나빠했어.

B: If only I could **apologize to** him. 내가 걔에게 사과할 수 있다면 좋을텐데.

get back to

영영 to return to something or someplace; to answer a message or missed call

의미 1. 되돌아가다 2. 다시 토의하다 3. 나중에 다시 얘기를 하다 4. 다시 연락하다(전화)

보충 get back to sth의 경우 …로 돌아가다, 다시 원점에서 토의하다

1. I'll **get back to** you on that. I might have other plans.
   그거 나중에 말해줄게. 다른 일이 있을지도 모르거든.

2. I got to **get back to** the bachelorette party.
   난 처녀파티에 다시 돌아가야 돼.

A: I'll **get back to** you when you're not so busy.
   바쁘시지 않을 때 다시 연락할게요.

B: If you catch me at the end of the day, I'll have more time to talk. 퇴근무렵에 전화하면 더 얘기할 수 있을 거예요.

afford to

영영 to be able to pay the full amount for something; to be able to do something without causing problems

의미 …할 여력이 있다

보충 주로 I can't afford+명사[to+V]의 형태로 쓰인다.

1. I can't **afford to** go on the ski trip next month.
   나 다음 달에 스키여행갈 여유가 안돼.

2. Can you **afford to** live in that apartment? 그 아파트에 살 여유가 돼?

A: I want to travel through Europe. 난 유럽일주 여행을 하고 싶어.

B: Can you **afford to** make that trip? 그 여행을 할 여유가 돼?

forget to

> **영영** to not remember, especially related to doing a task
>
> **의미** …할 것을 잊다
>
> **보충** Don't forget to do~ …을 명심해라, 잊지말고 해라

1. Don't **forget to** fill out those forms before you go.
   가기 전에 이 양식을 다 채우는 것 잊지마.

2. Please don't **forget to** make a backup of those files.
   그 파일의 복사본을 꼭 만들어 놓아.

A: It's your uncle's birthday. Don't **forget to** call him.
   삼촌 생신이야. 전화드리는 거 잊지마.

B: I'll do that right now. 지금 전화할게.

apply to

> **영영** to officially seek acceptance, particularly to a job or school; to relate to someone or something
>
> **의미** 1.(직장, 학교 등에) 지원하다 2. …와 관련이 있다 3.적용되다
>
> **보충** apply to+장소+for sth …에다 …을 지원[신청]하다, apply to+V …하기를 지원하다

1. Is it a good idea to **apply to** many colleges?
   많은 대학에 지원하는 게 좋은 생각이야?

2. That rule doesn't **apply to** us. 이 규칙은 우리에게 적용되지 않아.

A: I have to **apply to** get a visa for Australia. 호주 비자 신청을 해야 돼.

B: Are you going to attend school there? 거기 학교에 들어갈거야?

remember to

> **영영** to encourage someone not to forget, especially related to doing a task
>
> **의미** 앞으로 …할 것을 기억하다 *remember ~ing 과거에 …한 것을 기억하다
>
> **보충** remember sb ~ing …가 …한 것을 기억하다

1. I don't remember seeing you on the train. 열차에서 널 본 기억이 안나.

2. I distinctly remember you saying that you'd take care of the camera. 네가 사진기를 챙기겠다고 말한 걸 똑똑히 기억한다구.

A: Damn, I forgot a condom. 젠장, 콘돔 챙기는 걸 깜빡했어.

B: Just remember to keep it safe. 피임하는걸 명심하라고.

stop to

> **영영** to pause one thing in order to briefly do something else
>
> **의미** …하기 위해 멈추다 *stop ~ing …하는 것을 그만두다
>
> **보충** stop for sth …하기 위해 멈추다, can't stop ~ing 계속 …하다

1. We'll lose time if we stop to eat now.
   지금 먹기 위해 차를 세우면 시간을 잃을거야.

2. You have to stop smoking. It is going to kill you one day.
   너 담배 끊어야 돼. 언젠가 그 때문에 죽을거야.

A: Why are you slowing down? 왜 속도를 늦추는거야?

B: I've got to stop to use the toilet. 화장실가려고 멈춰야 돼.

agree to

영영 to accept someone's suggestion; to commit to do something

의미 …에 찬성하다(agree to sth), …하는거에 찬성하다(agree to+V)

1. I **agree to** be part of your project.　난 네 프로젝트에 참여하는데 동의해.
2. I was kind of surprised that you **agreed to** go on a blind date.
   난 네가 소개팅에 가기로 했다고 해서 좀 놀랐어.

A: Sandra made a lot of mistakes.　샌드라는 많은 실수를 했어.
B: She **agreed to** do a better job next time.
   다음에는 일을 더 잘하겠다고 동의했어.

commit to

영영 to promise or agree to a plan

의미 1.전념하다, 헌신하다　2.약속하다　3.충실하다

보충 make a commitment (to)~ 참여하다, 헌신하다, 전념하다

1. You've **committed to** raising a baby with her.
   넌 걔와 함께 아이를 키우는데 헌신했어.
2. Did he **make a commitment to** his girlfriend?
   걔 여친과 결혼약속을 했어?

A: So you only watch TV on certain nights?
   넌 특정한 날에만 TV를 본다는 말이지?
B: I'm **committed to** programs that are interesting.
   난 흥미있는 프로그램만 보고 있어.

occur to

> **영영** to have a sudden thought, to think of something
>
> **의미** 생각이나 아이디어가 순간적으로 갑자기 떠오르다
>
> **보충** It occurred to me that~ 혹은 It occurred to me to~의 두가지 형태로 쓰인다.

1. It didn't **occur to** me you would not be home.
   네가 집에 오지 않을거라는 생각은 들지 않았어.

2. It never **occurred to** me it could actually be true.
   그게 사실일 수도 있다는 생각이 전혀 들지 않았어.

A: What made you come back to the office? 왜 사무실로 돌아온거야?

B: It **occurred to** me that I had forgotten my cell phone.
   핸드폰을 놓고 온게 생각이 났어.

owe A to B

> **영영** to be obligated to repay someone
>
> **의미** 돈이나 도움을 …에게 빚지다(= owe sb sth, owe sth to sb)
>
> **보충** How much do I owe you? 얼마예요?

1. I **owe** my life **to** the man who saved me.
   난 나를 구해준 남자에게 목숨을 빚지고 있어.

2. I felt like I **owed** it **to** him. 이거 걔 덕택인 것 같아.

A: Why do you need to see Ray? 왜 레이를 만나야 돼?

B: He **owes** fifty dollars **to** me. 내게 50달러 빚졌거든.

Unit 01
Unit 02
Unit 03
Unit 04
Unit 05
Unit 06
Unit 07

go to work

영영 to travel to a job; to begin something

의미 1.출근하다 2.일을 시작하다 = get to work (+ to resume working)

보충 get (back) to work 다시 일을 시작하다, *get back to the office 사무실로 돌아가다

1. **I'm really sorry but I have to go to work.** 미안하지만 일하러가야 돼요.

2. **Yeah, well, get up. It's time to go to work.**
   그래, 일어나. 이제 일하러 가야지.

A: What time do you **go to work?** 몇시에 출근해?

B: I usually get to work at seven a.m. 난 보통 오전 7시에 출근해.

come close to

영영 to almost do something, to move nearer to something

의미 1.···에 가까이 가다(come close to+N)   2.거의 ···할 뻔하다(come close to+~ing)

1. **I didn't touch it, but I came close to it.**
   난 그것을 만지지는 않았지만 그거에 가까이 갔어.

2. **Has anyone ever come close to perfecting the formula?**
   누구 그 공식을 완성에 가까이 근접한 사람있어?

A: I had to stop running after 2 hours. 2시간 달린 후에 멈춰야 했어.

B: You **came close to** completing the marathon.
   거의 마라톤을 완주할 뻔했네.

can't stand to

- 영영 to hate or strongly dislike something
- 의미 …을 참을 수가 없다
- 보충 can't stand+명사[to+V, ~ing]

1. **I can hardly stand to** be with him. 난 걔랑 도저히 같이 못 다니겠어.
2. **I can't stand** that new guy at the office. 저 신입사원을 도저히 못보겠어.

A: **I can't stand** waiting in lines like this. 이렇게 줄서서 기다리는 건 못 참겠어.
B: Me, neither, do you want to leave? 나도 그래. 다른 데로 갈래?

get ready to

- 영영 to prepare, to be all set to start
- 의미 …할 준비가 되다 = be (all) set to+V
- 보충 be[get] ready to+V[for+명사]

1. **Are** you **ready to** order your meal yet? 식사 주문 준비되셨나요?
2. It's midnight and **I'm ready to** go to a club.
   자정이야, 난 클럽에 갈 준비가 됐어.

A: **Are** you **ready to** start our trip? 여행갈 준비됐어?
B: Yes, it seems like we can leave. 어, 출발해도 될 것 같아.

Unit 01
Unit 02
Unit 03
Unit 04
Unit 05
Unit 06
Unit 07

prefer A to B

> **영영** to express a choice of one thing over another
>
> **의미** …보다 …를 더 좋아하다, …하기를 더 좋아하다(prefer to+V)
>
> **보충** A, B의 형태는 명사, to+V, ~ing 모두 가능하다.

1. I **prefer** going out drinking **to** staying home.
난 집에 있는거보다 나가서 술마시고 싶어.

2. I **prefer to** be alone. Please leave. 난 혼자있는게 더 좋아. 나가줘.

A: Are you happy that you landed a new job? 새로운 일자리를 구해서 좋아?

B: I **prefer** working **to** being unemployed. 실업자보다는 일하는게 더 좋지.

can't wait to

> **영영** to look forward to something, to be impatient for something to occur
>
> **의미** 빨리 …하고 싶다(can't wait to+V[for+명사])
>
> **보충** = be eager to+V = be dying to+V

1. I **can't wait to** meet your dad this weekend!
이번 주말에 당신 아버님을 만나뵙는 게 너무 기다려져.

2. I **can't wait to** get out of here. 여기서 나가고 싶어 죽겠어.

A: I **can't wait** for the school holiday. 빨리 방학이 되었으면 해.

B: What will you do with your free time? 방학 때 뭐 할건데?

feel free to

> **영영** to have no hesitation or shyness in doing something
>
> **의미** 맘대로 …하다
>
> **보충** I want you to feel free to~ 네가 맘편히 …하도록 해, You can feel free to~ 마음편히 …해

1. **Feel free to** ask if you have any questions.
   무슨 궁금한 게 있으면 언제든 물어봐.

2. **Feel free to** stay here as long as you like.
   네가 원하는 만큼 부담없이 여기에 있어.

A: **Feel free to** stay here as long as you like.
   계시고 싶을 때까지 마음놓고 머무세요.

B: It's very kind of you to say so. 그렇게 말씀해주셔서 고맙습니다.

have to do with

> **영영** to be related to another thing; to have a relationship with someone or something else
>
> **의미** 관련이 있다, 관계가 있다(~with sb[sth])
>
> **보충** ↔ have nothing to do with

1. I think you **have something to do** with it.
   넌 그것과 무슨 관련이 있는 것 같아.

2. What does she **have to do with** this? 걔는 이거와 무슨 관련이 있어?

A: What does that **have to do with** the project?
   그게 그 프로젝트와 무슨 관련이 있어?

B: Nothing, but I thought it was interesting. 없어. 하지만 흥미롭다고 생각했어.

get married to

영영 to wed another person

의미 결혼하다 * be married는 결혼한 상태

보충 be married to John for 10 years 존과 결혼한지 10년 됐어, be getting married to sb on~ ···요일에 ··· 와 결혼해

1. My wife and I **have been married** for ten years.
   우리 부부는 결혼한지 10년 됐어.

2. Chris wanted to **get married to** me. 크리스는 나와 결혼하기를 바랬어.

A: Did you know Sheila **got married?** 쉴라가 결혼한 거 알고 있어?

B: No! When did that happen? 말도 안돼! 언제 한거야?

be supposed to

영영 to be expected or obligated to do something

의미 ···하기로 되어 있다, ···해야 한다

보충 be expected to~는 ···하기로 예상[기대]하다, ···하기로 되어 있다

1. She's **supposed to** arrive tomorrow after lunch.
   걔는 내일 점심 후에 도착하기로 되어 있어.

2. You're not **supposed to** hit on your teacher.
   선생님을 유혹해서는 안돼.

A: Do you know what time we're **supposed to** leave?
   우리가 몇 시에 떠나기로 되어있는지 아니?

B: Come to think of it I don't. 생각해 보니 모르겠는데.

make love to

> 영영 to engage in sex, especially in a romantic way
>
> 의미 사랑을 나누다

1. Can he **make love to** you all night long?
저 밤새 너랑 사랑을 나눌 수 있어?

2. The kids are away. I was sort of hoping we could **make love** tonight. 애들이 없으니 오늘 밤 우리가 좀 사랑을 나눌 수 있을까 바랬어.

A: That girl was pretty hot. 저 여자애 정말 섹시했어.

B: I **made love to** her all night long. 난 밤새내내 걔랑 사랑을 나누었어.

make it to

> 영영 to reach a specific point or destination
>
> 의미 제시간에 …에 도착하다
>
> 보충 make it 단독으로는 성공하다, 목표를 달성하다

1. I think we'll **make it to** the meeting.
내 생각에 우리는 회의에 맞춰 갈 수 있을 것 같아.

2. I won't be able to **make it to** the presentation.
발표회에 가지 못할 것 같아.

A: The festival is being held Saturday. 페스티발이 토요일날에 열려.

B: We can **make it to** that event. 거기에 갈 수 있겠다.

reply to

영영 to answer, often in either a spoken or written response

의미 응대하다, 답변하다

1. You'd better **reply to** this court summons.
   넌 법정소환에 답변을 해야 돼.

2. I forgot to **reply to** your e-mail.   네 이메일에 답하는 것을 잊었어.

A: Ryan never got back to me about the party.
   라이언은 파티에 관해 내게 답을 주지 않았어.

B: He often takes a long time to **reply to** invitations.
   걘 초대장에 답신하는데 종종 오래 걸려.

link to

영영 to connect one thing to another; to provide a connection to another website

의미 1.연결하다   2.웹사이트에 연결시키다, 링크를 걸어놓다

1. The robbery **was linked to** a criminal gang.
   그 절도는 한 범죄집단과 연결되어 있었어.

2. My website **is linked to** his podcast.
   내 웹사이트는 걔의 팟캐스트에 링크되어 있어.

A: I eat sausages or steak almost every day.
   난 거의 매일 소시지나 고기를 먹어.

B: Eating too much meat **has been linked to** cancer.
   고기를 너무 많이 먹는건 암과 연관되어 있어.

stick to

영영 to remain the same; to adhere and be attached to

의미 1.…을 계속하다, 고수하다 2.집중하다

보충 stick to sth

1. We made our decision. Let's just **stick to** it.
우린 결정을 했고 그걸 계속 고수하자고.

2. OK, **stick to** the facts. Don't lie to me.
좋아, 사실에 집중해. 거짓말하지 말고.

A: You should try to get a better job. 더 나은 직장을 얻도록 해봐.

B: I'm going to **stick to** working here. 난 여기서 계속 일할거야.

be with

영영 to be together, to accompany

의미 1.…와 함께 있다 2.…을 지지하다, …와 의견을 같이하다, …편이다

보충 I'm with you 알았어, 동감야, I'm with you there 그 점에 동의해

1. I can't wait to **be with** you! 너랑 빨리 함께 있고 싶어!

2. **I'm with** you all the way! Let's go talk to him.
전적으로 당신 편이에요! 걔한테 얘기하러 갑시다.

A: He's really bad at following directions. 그 사람은 교통법규를 정말 안 지켜.

B: That's why I always drive when **I'm with** him.
그래서 함께 가면 항상 내가 운전하잖아.

agree with

- **영영** to think something is correct or accurate
- **의미** 동의하다, 찬성하다
- **보충** agree with sth, agree with sb (about sth)

1. I **agree with** everything you said. 네가 말한 모든 거에 동의해.
2. The others didn't **agree with** me. 다른 사람들은 나에게 동의하지 않았어.

A: I think we should go and celebrate. 가서 축하하자.

B: I entirely **agree with** you. 전적으로 동감이야.

stay with

- **영영** to remain, to be together without changing
- **의미** 1.…와 함께 머물다 2.…의 집에 묵다 3.어렵거나 원치 않는 일이지만 계속하다(stay with sth)

1. Is it okay if we still **stay with** you tonight?
   오늘밤 너와 함께 있어도 괜찮아?
2. She **has been staying with** her mom in Chicago.
   걘 시카고에서 엄마와 함께 머무르고 있어.

A: I'd like you to **stay with** me tonight. 오늘 밤 안 갔으면 좋겠어.

B: I can be a little longer but I have to go home at 12.
   더 있을 수 있지만 12시에는 집에 가야 돼.

go with

영영 to accompany, to move in the same direction together

의미 1.…와 함께 가다 2.포함되다 3.어울리다 4.선택하다

보충 go with sb 함께 가다, 연애하다, go with sth 포함되다, 어울리다, 선택하다

1. Would you like me to **go with** you? 너랑 함께 갈까?

2. I think our clients are going to **go with** another company.
고객들이 타사와 거래할 것 같아.

A: This coffee tastes great. 커피 맛 좋네.

B: Let me get you a piece of pie to **go with** it.
커피랑 같이 먹도록 파이 한 조각 갖다줄게.

meet with

영영 to purposefully gather together; to unexpectedly come upon; to unexpectedly happen

의미 1.논의하기 위해서 만나다 2.우연히 만나다

보충 meet with는 다소 formal, meet up with하면 캐주얼한 표현이 난다.

1. I'm afraid to **meet with** the principal. 교장선생님을 만나는게 두려워.

2. We're very grateful that you agreed to **meet with** us.
이렇게 만나줘서 정말 감사해요.

A: Why are you so nervous? 왜 그렇게 초조해 하는거야?

B: I have to **meet with** my boss. 사장과 만나야 돼.

check with

영영 to ask for permission; to make certain something is accurate or true

의미 1.물어보다 2.확인하다

보충 check with sb about sth …에게 …에 관해 물어보다

1. Did you **check with** security? 경비에게 확인했어?
2. **Check with** me about stuff like this. 이런 일은 내게 물어봐.

A: Come on, join us for dinner. 그러지말고 저녁식사 같이 하자.

B: I've got to **check with** my wife first. 먼저 아내에게 확인해야 돼.

help with

영영 to assist in doing something; to make easier

의미 도와주다(help with sth), …가 …하는 것을 도와주다(help sb with~[V])

1. You promised to **help with** my project.
   내 프로젝트 도와주기로 약속했잖아.

2. Let me **help** you **with** your baggage.
   짐드는거 도와줄게요.

A: Is there something we can **help with**? 우리가 뭐 도와줄게 있어?

B: No, just sit back and relax. 아니. 그냥 앉아서 쉬어.

do with

- **영영** to prefer to have something
- **의미** …을 어떻게 하다, with 이하를 어떻게 하다
- **보충** What're we going to do with~? 우리 …을 어떻게 하지?, What did you do with~? …를 어떻게 한거야?

1. What will you **do with** your extra money? 여유 돈으로 뭘 할거야?

2. What are you going to **do with** her when she gets here?
   걔가 여기 오면 걔를 어떻게 할거야?

A: What are you going to **do with** the offer? 그 제안을 어떻게 할거야?

B: I'm pretty sure I'm going to turn it down. 거절하게 될 게 분명해.

mess with

- **영영** to make something disorderly, to cause problems
- **의미** 1.쓸데없이 간섭하다   2.건드리다
- **보충** mess with sb 쓸데없이 간섭하다, 속이거나 말썽을 일으키다, mess with sth 안좋은 일에 관여하다

1. I'm a dangerous man. You don't wanna **mess with** me.
   나 위험한 남자야. 건드리지마.

2. Why do you want to **mess with** that? 왜 넌 그걸 망쳐놓고 싶은거야?

A: Chris is walking around looking mean.
   크리스는 더러운 표정을 지으며 걸어가고 있어.

B: He's angry, so don't **mess with** him. 걔 열받았으니 건들지마.

deal with

> 영영 to give attention to something, often to solve a problem; to tolerate or endure
>
> 의미 1.처리하다, 다루다   2.감당하다
>
> 보충 I can deal with it 감당할 수 있어, 처리할 수 있어, 그래 가능해

1. There is no time to **deal with** this mess. 이 혼란을 처리할 시간이 없어.

2. The teacher had to **deal with** a troubled student.
   선생님은 사고친 학생을 다루어야 했어.

A: This computer has been broken for a week.
   이 컴퓨터는 일주일간 고장 나 있었어.

B: I can **deal with** it. It's not hard to fix the problem.
   내가 처리할 수 있어. 수리하는 게 어렵지 않아.

be busy with

> 영영 to be hard at work with something, to be engaged in something
>
> 의미 …으로 바쁘다
>
> 보충 be busy with sth[~ing] 혹은 be busy ~ing

1. I **was too busy** keeping an eye on the kids.
   난 아이들 돌보는데 너무 바빴어.

2. I'm **busy with** making my breakfast.
   내 아침 먹을거 준비하느라 바빠.

A: I haven't seen you much lately.   최근에 많이 못봤네.

B: I've **been busy with** family stuff.   가족문제로 바빴어.

be finished with

영영 to have completed something; to give up or quit something, to end

의미 …을 끝내다, 마치다 = finish+명사[~ing]

보충 be finished with sb 관계가 끝나다, 관련업무가 끝나다

1. **I'm not finished with** the report. 보고서 작성 아직 못 끝냈어.

2. **Are** you **finished with** him? 너 개랑 끝났어?

A: When can we go home? 우리 언제 집에 갈 수 있어?

B: After we're **finished with** this project. 이 프로젝트를 끝낸 후에.

be done with

영영 to have completed something; to end or quit something

의미 1. …을 끝내다, 처리하다 2. (음식) 다 먹다 3. 헤어지다(with sb)

보충 You done? 다했어?, 다 끝냈어?

1. **I am done with** cleaning up this house! 이 집 청소하는거 끝냈어.

2. I can't understand these directions. **I'm done with** this!
이 지시사항을 이해 못하겠어. 그만할테야!

A: Can I take away your plate? 접시 치울까?

B: No, I'm **not done with** my snacks. 아니, 과자 아직 다 못먹었어.

argue with

> **영영** to express disagreement between two people, to verbally fight
>
> **의미** 언쟁하다, 싸우다

1. Did you **argue with** him? Was there a fight? 걔랑 다퉜어? 싸웠어?
2. You really want to **argue with** me about this?
   너 정말 나랑 이거갖고 말다툼할거야?

A: I think Mindy is the prettiest girl in our class.
   민디가 우리 반에서 가장 이쁜 것 같아.

B: I won't **argue with** that. 두말하면 잔소리지.

live with

> **영영** to have a home with a person, often with a sexual relationship; to endure or tolerate, especially something unpleasant
>
> **의미** 1.함께 살다   2.불쾌한 것을 참다, 견디다

1. I want to **live with** you too! Let's do that!
   나도 너랑 함께 살고 싶어! 그렇게 하자!
2. How will I **live with** the shame? 내가 어떻게 그 치욕을 견딜까?

A: Willie was in a serious accident. 윌리가 큰 사고를 당했어.

B: He'll have to **live with** those injuries for a long time.
   평생 그 상처를 안고 살아가야 될거야.

think about

영영 to consider something; to take time to make a decision

의미 …에 대해서 생각하다

1. I haven't had much time to **think about** it.
난 그거에 대해 생각할 시간이 많지 않았어.

2. I can't help but **think about** Lisa. 리사 생각을 떨쳐버릴 수가 없어.

A: I want to invite the investors to see our operation.
투자가들을 불러서 우리 회사를 둘러보게 하는 게 좋겠어.

B: Let me **think about** that and I'll get back to you.
생각 좀 해보고 얘기해 줄게.

know about

영영 to have information or knowledge of something, to be aware of

의미 …에 대해 들어서 알고 있다

1. I don't **know about** the new plans. 새 계획에 대해서는 몰라.

2. What do you want to **know about** Angela?
안젤라에 대해 뭘 알고 싶어?

A: Could you give me some advice about real estate?
부동산에 관해서 조언 좀 해줄래?

B: Sorry. I don't **know about** that. 미안해. 부동산에 대해서는 아는 게 없어.

hear about

영영 to learn new information about something

의미 …에 대한 소식을 듣다 = hear of, …가 …한다는 얘기를 듣다(hear about sb ~ing)

보충 Did you hear about~? …에 대한 얘기 들어 알고 있어?

1. I **heard about** you getting married next month.
네가 다음 달에 결혼한다는 이야기 들었어.

2. She doesn't want to **hear about** your life history.
걘 네 인생사에 대해 듣고 싶지 않아 해.

A: Did you **hear about** the plans for the new stadium?
새로운 경기장 계획에 대해 들어봤어?

B: It is supposed to be built in this neighborhood. 이 지역에 세워질거래.

forget about

영영 to not recall something; to purposefully not think about something; to accidentally not remember some obligation

의미 …을 잊다, 깜박하다

보충 forget about+명사[~ing]

1. **Forget about** your problems. 네 문제들을 잊어.

2. I **forgot about** paying those bills. 저 고지서 돈내는 것을 잊어버렸어.

A: The new secretary is hot, but she's a lesbian!
새로운 비서 죽이던데, 그 여자 레즈비언이야!

B: I guess I can **forget about** going out with her!
데이트 할 생각은 잊어버려야겠구나.

worry about

영영 to be stressed or concerned about something

의미 걱정하다

보충 worry about~ = be worried about~

1. You should **worry about** your future more.
넌 미래를 좀 더 걱정해야지.

2. I'm so **worried** that I might fail the exam. 시험에 떨어질까봐 너무 걱정돼.

A: Jim and Erin have a strange relationship. 짐하고 에린은 관계가 이상해.

B: I'm **worried about** them fighting too much.
걔네들이 너무 많이 싸우는게 걱정돼.

care about

영영 to have affection for someone or something, to be concerned with

의미 관심을 갖거나 중요하다고 생각해 신경을 쓰다, 좋아하다

1. No one seemed to **care about** her feelings.
아무도 걔 감정에 대해서는 신경쓰지도 않는 것 같았어.

2. I **care about** what people think of me.
난 사람들이 나에 대해서 하는 말에 맘을 써.

A: Your friends say you've been acting strange.
네 친구들이 그러던데 너 좀 이상하게 행동한다며.

B: I don't **care about** what they think. 걔네들이 뭐라 생각하든 상관없어.

inquire about

영영 to ask about someone or something

의미 어떤 정보를 알고자 문의하다

보충 inquire into~ 조사하다, inquire after~ …의 안부를 묻다

1. I'm not gonna **inquire about** that right now.
   지금은 더이상 그것에 대해 묻지 않을게.

2. John **inquired about** a new job. 존은 새로운 일자리에 대해 문의를 했어.

A: What did that man want? 저 남자가 뭘 원한거야?

B: He wanted to **inquire about** a car I'm selling.
   내가 팔려는 차에 대해 물어보고 싶어했어.

complain about

영영 to express unhappiness or dissatisfaction with someone or something

의미 불평하다, 항의하다

보충 complain about[of]~, complain to sb …에게 항의하다

1. I'm here to **complain about** the noise. 시끄럽다고 항의하러 왔는데요.

2. I'd like to **complain about** the parking attendant.
   주차요원에 대해 항의하려구요.

A: Brian is really unhappy working there.
   브라이언은 거기서 일하는걸 정말 안좋아해.

B: I've never heard him **complaining about** anything.
   브라이언이 뭐 불평하는 것을 들어본 적이 없는데.

bring about

> **영영** to cause to happen, to happen as the result of an earlier event
>
> **의미** 야기시키다, 일으키다

1. That might **bring about** big trouble.

그로 인해 큰 어려움이 야기될 수도 있어.

2. Linda's diet **brought about** weight loss.

린다는 다이어트를 해서 몸무게를 뺐어.

A: Do you think it's a good idea to get married? 결혼하는게 좋은 생각같아?

B: It will **bring about** big changes in your life.

네 인생에 커다란 변화가 생길거야.

come about

> **영영** to occur, to happen
>
> **의미** 일어나다, 발생하다

1. I expected to be promoted, but it never **came about**.

승진예상을 했는데 그러지 못했어.

2. The changes are expected to **come about** this afternoon.

그 변화가 오늘 오후에 일어날거라 예상되고 있어.

A: There are plans for a new shopping center here.

여기에 새로운 쇼핑센터 세울 계획이 있어.

B: That will take years to **come about**. 그러려면 수년은 걸릴거야.

get about

영영 to go to various places, especially to be social with others

의미 돌아다니다, 퍼지다

1. She may be old, but she still **gets about.**
그녀는 나이가 들었을지 몰라도 여전히 돌아다니셔.

2. I wasn't able to **get about** when I was sick.
아플 때면 돌아다닐 수가 없어.

A: My car is broken and I don't like riding the bus.
내 자동차가 망가졌고 난 버스타는 것을 싫어해.

B: So how do you **get about**? 그럼 어떻게 돌아다니냐?

tweet about

영영 to write opinions online in a fast, short manner on twitter

의미 트윗을 보내다(send out tweets)

1. Someone **tweeted about** a party tonight.
오늘 파티에 대해 누가 트윗을 날렸어.

2. Do you plan to **tweet about** our argument?
우리 논쟁에 대해 트윗에 올릴거야?

A: For some reason, Don sends out tweets every day.
무슨 이유인지 모르겠지만 돈은 매일 트윗해.

B: I hate it when he **tweets about** stupid things.
걔가 말도 안되는 얘기를 트윗할 때 짜증나.

over·from

over
가로질러, …에 대해, 끝난 ex. go over, be over

off
제거, 분리, 정지 ex. take off, pull off

back
다시 뒤로, 뒤에서 ex. pay back, give back

from
근거, 분리, 기원, 이유 ex. come from

at
…에, 목표, 기간, 원인 ex. look at

go over

영영 to occur; to travel to a place; to review or look at something; to travel on top of something

의미 1.자세히 검토하다, 조사하다 2.…으로[위로] 가다 3.반복하다

보충 go over to sb[sth] to+V …로 가서 …을 하다

1. I'd appreciate it if you could **go over** these figures with me.
나와 함께 이 수치들을 검토해 준다면 정말 고맙겠는데.

2. Would you like me to **go over** it again with you?
내가 다시 얘기해줄까?

A: Can we **go over** this paperwork? 우리 이 서류를 검토할 수 있을까?

B: Sure, let's start on page one. 물론, 1페이지부터 시작하자.

be over

영영 to finish; to visit someone; to be on top of

의미 1.끝나다, 끝내다 2.방문하다

보충 be over+수 …수치를 넘다, be all over sb는 be over의 강조형, 혹은 이성에게 들이대다

1. When I said it**'s over**, I meant we're breaking up.
내가 끝났다고 말했을 때 내 말은 헤어졌다는거였어.

2. You just have to hang in there until it **is all over.**
모든 게 끝날 때까지 참고 견뎌야 돼.

A: Our relationship **is over.** It's finished. 우리 관계는 끝났어. 끝났다고.

B: I understand we can't go out anymore.
이제 더 이상 우리는 데이트는 못하겠구만.

think over

> 영영 to consider, usually in order to reach a decision
>
> 의미 뭔가 결정하기에 앞서 심사숙고하다
>
> 보충 think over+제안명사(offer, proposal, suggestion)

1. Take some time to **think over** our offer.
   시간을 좀 갖고 우리의 제의를 생각해봐.

2. **Think over** everything you've been told.
   네가 들은 거 모든 것을 신중하게 검토해봐.

A: Will you come to work for my company? 우리 회사에서 일하시겠어요?

B: Let me have some time to **think** it **over**. 좀 생각해볼 시간을 주십시오.

check over

> 영영 to look at to find mistakes; to look for potential problems
>
> 의미 제대로 되어있는지, 틀린 것은 없는지 철저히 조사하다, 확인하다

1. I **checked over** the place but didn't see her.
   난 그곳을 철저히 조사해봤지만 걔를 보지 못했어.

2. I'm **checking over** the report for mistakes.
   난 그 보고서에 실수가 있는지 자세히 보고 있는 중야.

A: Why do you need a lawyer? 왜 변호사가 필요해?

B: I want him to **check over** the divorce agreement.
   이혼합의서를 철저히 검토하기 위해서.

get over

영영 to recover from or overcome a difficulty, especially a sad or bad experience or illness

의미 안 좋은 일이나 곤란한 상황을 이겨내다

보충 get over sb 헤어진 후 잊다, get over (with) (다른 일을 하기 위해) 빨리 해치우다, 끝내버리다

1. You'd better **get over** your bad mood. 넌 우울한 감정을 이겨내도록 해.

2. Well, I think I can help you **get over** him.
   글쎄 네가 걔랑 끝내는 거 도와줄 수 있을 것 같아.

A: My wife's a little shaken up. 내 아내가 좀 충격을 받았어.

B: Don't worry, she'll **get over** it in a few weeks.
   걱정마, 몇 주 후면 괜찮아질거야.

hand over

영영 to give something to someone else, usually something considered very important; to pass a responsibility to someone else

의미 1.중요한 것을 건네주다 2.책임을 다른 사람에게 전가하다

1. I expect the lawyer to **hand over** my documents.
   난 변호사가 내 서류들을 건네줄거라 생각했어.

2. The prisoner **was handed over to** the police officers.
   그 죄수는 경찰관에서 인도되었어.

A: You can take my car to work. 내차 갖고 출근해.

B: Great. **Hand over** your keys. 좋아. 키 좀 줘.

Unit 01
Unit 02
Unit 03
Unit 04
Unit 05
Unit 06
Unit 07

pull over

> **영영** to stop by the side of the road; to cause someone to stop by the side of the road as a police officer
>
> **의미** 사람을 내려주기 위해 차를 길가에 대다, 단속에 걸려 길가에 차를 대다
>
> **보충** pull up은 신호등 정지선 혹은 주차장 등에 차를 세우다

1. Just **pull over** and let me out of the car! 차를 세우고 날 내려줘!
2. She **got pulled over** for speeding. 걘 속도위반으로 단속에 걸렸어.

A: Holy cow! The car is on fire. 이런! 차에 불이 붙었어.

B: Hurry up and **pull over**. 빨리 차를 길 한 쪽에 세워.

look over

> **영영** to gaze in a certain direction; to examine carefully for details or mistakes
>
> **의미** 주의깊게 검토하다, 살펴보다
>
> **보충** look over+장소명사 …에 가보다, …를 살펴보다

1. Feel free to have your lawyer **look** it **over**.
   마음편히 네 변호사에게 그거 검토해보라고 해.

2. The police **looked over** the crime scene. 경찰은 범죄현장을 살펴봤어.

A: Do you want to **look over** the menu? 메뉴판을 볼래?

B: No, I know what I want to eat. 아니, 뭘 먹고 싶은지 아는데.

come over

> **영영** to go to another place, often as a social visit; to be affected by a change of mood
>
> **의미** 1.…로 가다 2.들르다 3.(감정 등이) …을 사로잡다
>
> **보충** come over to one's place …의 집에 들르다

1. I need you to **come over** here at 5 p.m. tomorrow.
내일 오후 5시에 여기로 와주셨으면 해요.

2. Can you **come over** to my house? 우리집에 잠시 들를래?

A: Do you want to **come over** to my place tonight? 오늘밤 우리 집에 올래?

B: Sure, what time is good for you? 그래, 몇 시가 좋아?

stay over

> **영영** to spend the night somewhere
>
> **의미** 1.머무르다 2.하룻밤 묵다, 외박하다

1. We'll **stay over** till he shows up. 우린 걔가 올 때까지 기다릴거야.

2. I've got to get up really early, so you can't **stay over.**
난 정말 일찍 일어나야 하니까 넌 자고 갈 수가 없어.

A: It's getting too snowy to drive. 차를 몰기에는 눈이 너무 오네.

B: Maybe we should **stay over** in a hotel. 호텔에 머물러야 될지 모르겠네.

Unit 01
Unit 02
Unit 03
Unit 04
Unit 05
Unit 06
Unit 07

invite over

영영 to ask someone to visit your home

의미 집으로 술이나 식사를 하게 …을 초대하다(invite sb over for sth)

보충 invite sb out for sth 집밖으로 초대하다, invite sb to[for] sth …에 초대하다

1. Next time, don't **invite** her **to** the party.
   다음번에는 걔를 파티에 초대하지마.

2. She **invited** me **over** for dinner. 걘 저녁먹자고 날 초대했어.

A: Did you meet our new neighbors? 새로운 우리 이웃들 만났어?

B: No. Let's **invite** them **over** for coffee. 아니. 커피마시자고 초대하자.

tide ~over

영영 to be enough for right now, to be adequate for a short time; to be enough to last through a difficult period

의미 1.…가 어려움을 이겨내도록 돕다   2.당장은 …하기에 충분하다

1. The food will **tide** them **over**. 음식으로 걔네들은 힘든 시기를 이겨낼거야.

2. There's not enough beer to **tide** me **over**.
   내 갈증을 이겨낼 맥주가 충분히 없어.

A: Have you got enough money? 돈은 충분히 가지고 있어?

B: I think it's enough to **tide** us **over**.
   우리가 힘든 시기를 넘기기에는 충분할 것 같아.

blow over

> 영영 to be done with a difficult time; to be done with a big storm
>
> 의미 1. (어려움) 지나다, 사그라들다   2. 폭풍이 잦아들다

1. Stay calm and this will **blow over**.   진정해, 이거 사그라들거야.

2. The storm **blew over** after the rain fell.
   폭풍은 비가 내린 후에 잦아들었어.

A: There is a major political scandal going on.
   커다란 정치적 추문이 돌고 있어.

B: I'm sure it will **blow over** in a few weeks.   몇 주 후면 잦아들거야.

fall over

> 영영 to collapse to the ground
>
> 의미 바닥에 넘어지다

1. Mike punched her and the waitress **fell over**.
   마이크가 여종업원을 한대 때리니까 걔가 넘어졌어.

2. The tree **fell over** during the wind storm.
   그 나무는 폭풍이 부는 동안 쓰러졌어.

A: What happened when Jim had a heart attack?
   짐이 심장마비가 왔을 때 어떻게 됐어?

B: He put his hand to his chest and **fell over**.   걘 가슴에 손을 대고 쓰러졌어.

take over

영영 to get control of something, to become the new leader

의미 떠맡다, 맡아주다, 인수하다(새로운 리더가 되다)

1. Can you **take over** for me, please? 내 대신 맡아줄테야?
2. So then you just **took over** his business?
   그래서 그냥 그 사람의 사업체를 양도받은거야?

A: Mr. Johnson is retiring next year. 존슨 씨는 내년에 정년퇴직해.

B: Who will **take over** when he's gone? 그가 가면 누가 그 자리를 맡을까?

pass over

영영 to overlook; to choose someone or something else instead

의미 1.무시하다, …의 가치를 알아주지 않다   2.대신 …을 선택하다

1. I was hoping my book would be considered, but they **passed it over.** 내 책이 (상 등을) 받을만한 것 같은데 사람들이 알아주지 않아.
2. Don't **pass over** this proposal, because it's good.
   이 제안을 무시하지마, 좋은 제안이거든.

A: Were you offered a promotion at work? 직장에서 승진을 제의받았어?

B: Unfortunately, I **was passed over** again. 불행하게도, 난 또 탈락했어.

get off

> **영영** to exit, especially something that was taller or moving; to enjoy sexual pleasure
>
> **의미** 1.(버스나 열차에서) 내리다   2.퇴근하다   3.오르가즘에 오르다
>
> **보충** get down on(오럴섹스를 하다), get it on(섹스하다), get a hard-on(발기하다 = get hard)

1. He watches porn to **get off**. 갠 사정하기 위해서 포르노를 봐.
2. I **got hard** just looking at her. 난 걔를 쳐다보기만 해도 발기가 돼.

A: You guys were in bed for a long time. 너희들 오랫동안 침대에 있었어.

B: It takes him a while to **get off**. 걔가 사정하는데 꽤 걸렸어.

take off

> **영영** to remove; to leave; to take flight, as with a plane or rocket
>
> **의미** 1.제거하다   2.떠나다, 가다   3.이륙하다   4.쉬다   5.옷을 벗다(↔ put on)
>
> **보충** need some time off 휴가가 좀 필요하다

1. You're saying you need to **take** a day **off**. 하루 쉬고 싶다는거지.
2. We're about to **take off** and see a movie. 우리 지금 나가서 영화보려고.

A: I haven't seen Andy at work. 사무실에서 앤디가 안보이는데.

B: He **took** some time **off** to relax. 쉴려고 좀 휴가를 냈어.

drop off

영영 to transport someone to a destination; to allow to fall; to diminish or taper off

의미 1.(차 등) 내려주다 …까지 태워주다   2.떨어트리다   3.줄어들다

1. Can you **drop off** Billy on the way home?
   너 집에 오는 길에 빌리를 내려줄 수 있어?

2. Could you do me a favor and **drop** me **off** after work?
   부탁해도 될까? 퇴근 후에 차 좀 태워줄래?

A: I would be happy to **drop** you **off** at the subway.
   널 전철역까지 태워다줄게.

B: That's very kind of you.   고맙기도 해라.

pay off

영영 to give money that is owed; to secretly give money illegally to hide legal or ethical problems

의미 1.빚을 갚다   2.보상받다   3.성과를 내다   4.뇌물을 주다

1. Are you sure you can **pay off** our debts?
   우리 빚을 확실히 갚을 수 있어?

2. I knew all that hard work would **pay off** someday.
   열심히 일하면 언젠가 성과가 나타나는건 당연한거지.

A: I thought it was illegal to have a business here.
   여기서 영업하는 것은 불법이라 생각해.

B: I heard they have to **pay off** the cops.   경찰에게 뇌물을 줘야 한다고 들었어.

show off

영영 to make a big display of personal abilities or wealth in order to show superiority, often in a way that annoys other people

의미 짜증나게 자랑질을 하다, 과시하다(boast)

보충 show-off 자랑질하는 사람

1. It makes people angry when you **show off**.
네가 과시할 때 사람들이 열받어.

2. She's a bit of **a show-off,** but she gets the job done.
좀 잘난 척 하지만 자기 일은 잘해.

A: Why did Bob come to your house? 왜 밥이 네 집에 온거야?

B: He wanted to **show off** his new car. 걘 새로 뽑은 자기 차를 자랑하고 싶어했어.

see off

영영 to go with someone to a taxi, a port, an airport, or a train or bus station, to say goodbye as they leave

의미 택시, 공항이나 정거장 등에 가서 떠나는 사람을 배웅하다

보충 문밖에서 배웅하는 것은 see out

1. Did anyone **see** Brad **off** before the trip?
브래드가 여행가기 전에 배웅한 사람있어?

2. How many people came to **see** you **off?**
널 배웅하러 몇 사람이 나온거야?

A: So your sister is going to France? 그래 네 누나가 프랑스에 간다고?

B: We're going to **see** her **off** at the airport. 공항에서 배웅할거야.

put off

> **영영** to delay or postpone something; to do something that upsets others; to confuse
>
> **의미** 1.연기하다 2.다른 사람 화나게 할 일을 하다 3.혼란하게 하다
>
> **보충** put off+명사[~ing]

1. He shouldn't **have put off** finishing the work.
   걘 일끝내는 걸 미루지 말았어야 했는데.

2. My son always **puts off** doing homework. 내 아들은 항상 숙제를 미뤄.

A: The doctor diagnosed me with cancer. 의사가 내가 암이라고 진단했어.

B: You can't **put off** getting treatment. 치료받는 것을 늦추면 안돼.

run off (with)

> **영영** to take something unexpectedly; to steal; to unexpectedly leave one relationship or marriage in order to be with someone else
>
> **의미** 1.몰래 갖고 튀다(run off with sth) 2.눈이 맞아 몰래 달아나다(run off with sb)
>
> **보충** run off to~ …로 뛰어가다, …하러 급히가다

1. I just have to **run off** to the bathroom. 난 화장실로 뛰어가야 했어.

2. She's not going to divorce Chris and **run off** with you.
   걘 크리스와 이혼하고 너와 달아나지 않을거야.

A: His family used to be very wealthy. 그의 가족은 매우 잘 살았어.

B: Their accountant **ran off** with all of their money.
   그 집 회계사가 그들 돈을 몰래 다 갖고 튀었어.

shut off

> **영영** to cause something to stop, to switch off the power
> **의미** 멈추게 하다, 전원을 끄다

1. If you **shut off** the TV, then we can concentrate.
네가 TV를 끄면 우리는 집중할 수 있어.

2. **Shut off** the faucet when you leave the bathroom.
화장실에서 나올 때 꼭지를 잠궈라.

A: Did you **shut off** the lights in the living room? 거실 전등불 껐어?

B: No, sorry, I forgot to do that. 아니, 미안, 깜박했어.

piss off

> **영영** to make angry, to annoy
> **의미** 열받게 하다, 화나게 하다
> **보충** be pissed off (with/at+N) (…에게) 열받다. Piss off! 꺼져!

1. You really know how to **piss off** people.
넌 정말 사람 열받게 하는데 재주가 있어.

2. **She's not pissed at** Steve, **She's pissed at** me.
걔는 스티브가 아니라 나한테 화가 난거야.

A: Chris **has really pissed off** the boss.
크리스가 사장에게 정말 화를 많이 내더라고.

B: I say he quits this week. 이번주에 걔 그만둔다니까.

hit it off

영영 to like mutually a short time after meeting, to enjoy the company of

의미 만나자마자 바로 친해지다, 죽이 잘 맞다

1. We really **hit it off** when we met. 우리가 만났을 때 정말 죽이 잘 맞았어.
2. Did you **hit it off** with your new co-worker?
   새로운 동료와 죽이 잘 맞았어?

A: Sam and Chris have been talking all night. 샘과 크리스는 밤새 이야기했어.

B: It looks like they really **hit it off**. 정말 서로 죽이 잘 맞는 것 같아.

back off

영영 to retreat, to step away from a confrontation; to allow distance between

의미 1.뒤로 물러서다, 대립을 피하다 2.진정하다

1. I'm not talking to you. **Back off!** 너한테 말하는 거 아냐. 꺼져!
2. If she doesn't want to talk, you **back off.**
   만약 걔가 말하고 싶지 않아 한다면 넌 좀 물러서.

A: Kelly is still refusing to talk to me. 켈리는 여전히 나하고 얘기하지 않으려고 해.

B: It's best to **back off** and let her calm down.
   뒤로 물러나 걔가 진정하도록 하는게 최선이야.

call off

> 영영 to cancel, to shut down
> 의미 취소하다, 멈추다
> 보충 call off the meeting 회의를 취소하다

1. I want you to **call off** the wedding. 네가 결혼식을 취소하라고.
2. She told me that Jim **called off** his engagement with Jessica.
   걔가 그러는데 짐은 제시카와 파혼했대.

A: I thought the company was hosting a banquet.
   회사가 연회를 연다고 생각했는데.
B: It **was called off** because of the expense. 경비 때문에 취소됐어.

break off

> 영영 to stop a planned action; to divide from something larger
> 의미 1.(관계 등을) 끝내다, 중단하다   2.본체로부터 떨어져 나가다
> 보충 break it off with sb = break up with sb …와 헤어지다

1. Why did you **break off** your wedding engagement?
   왜 혼사를 깬거야?
2. My father **broke off** his affair with Nancy.
   아버지는 낸시와의 관계를 정리하셨어.

A: Jeff punched me for no reason. 제프가 아무 이유없이 나를 때렸어.
B: You should **break off** your relationship with him.
   너 걔하고 관계를 정리해야겠다.

kick off

> **영영** to begin something; to start certain sports matches like soccer and American football
>
> **의미** 축구에서 시작을 알리는 킥오프를 하듯 어떤 회의나 행사를 시작하다
>
> **보충** kick sb off 쫓아내다

1. The festival will **kick off** with a fireworks display.
   축제가 불꽃놀이와 함께 시작될거야.

2. **The kick off** for the soccer match is at 7. 축구경기 시작은 7시야.

A: It's the beginning of another year. 또다른 한 해의 시작이네.

B: Let's **kick off** the new year by getting drunk!
   술취하는 걸로 한해를 시작하자!

lay off

> **영영** to halt or stop something; to fire workers because the company does not need them
>
> **의미** 1.짜증나게 하는 것을 그만두다   2.근로자들을 일시 해고하다

1. Can you **lay off** please? I know I'm late.
   그만 좀 하실래요? 늦은 거 안다구요.

2. We're going to have to **lay off** at least twenty people.
   우리가 최소한 20명은 해고를 하게 될거야.

A: You're always drinking, and you spend too much money.
   너 맨날 술타령이고 돈을 너무 많이 써.

B: **Lay off** of me, alright? I'm tired. 나 좀 내버려둘래. 어? 피곤하다.

rip off

> **영영** to trick or cheat out of money; to pull something off quickly or violently
>
> **의미** 1.훔치다(rip sth off) 2.바가지 씌우다, 사기치다(rip sb off)
>
> **보충** rip-off 바가지 씌워서 산 제품

1. They **ripped** you **off** when you bought that.
너 그거 살 때 바가지 쓴거야.

2. Some car salesmen **rip off** their customers.
일부 차 세일즈맨들은 고객들에게 바가지를 씌워.

A: This phone cost over $300. 이 폰은 300 달러 이상이야.

B: You **got ripped off.** It's only worth half that.
너 바가지 쓴거야. 반가격밖에 안하는거야.

pull off

> **영영** to do something that was very difficult; to yank or use force to get something away from something else
>
> **의미** 1.어려운 일을 해내다, 성공하다 2.힘을 써서 떼어놓다

1. I can't believe you **pulled off** that trick. 네가 그런 트릭을 해낼 줄이야.

2. Can you **pull off** the tag on my dress? 내 옷에서 태그 좀 떼어줄래?

A: Your brother got a perfect score on the exam?
네 오빠가 시험에서 100점을 받았다고?

B: It was difficult, but he **pulled it off.** 어렵지만 해냈어.

call back

영영 to respond to a telephone message; to summon; to be interviewed a second time

의미 1.다시 전화하다(call again) 2.답신 전화를 하다 = return one's call, 부르다

1. Please tell him to **call back** after lunch.
   점심 후에 걔보고 전화하라고 해줘.

2. I'll have her **call** you **back** as soon as she gets in.
   걔가 들어오는 대로 전화하라고 할게.

A: Any messages for me? 나한테 온 메시지있어?

B: Your lawyer called and he wants you to **call back.**
   변호사한테 전화왔었는데 전화해달래.

bring back

영영 to transport to where something originated, to return something

의미 1.돌려주다 2.다시 데려다주다 3.…을 기억나게 하다

보충 bring sth back for sb. 혹은 bring sb back sth …에게 …을 돌려주다

1. **Bring** that **back** when you're done with it, OK?
   그거 다 쓰고나면 가져와, 알았지?

2. There's no guarantee the surgery's going to **bring back** your memory. 수술해도 기억이 되살아나는 걸 보증하지 않아.

A: I want you to **bring back** a snack. 과자 좀 가지고 와.

B: Really? What do you want to eat? 정말? 어떤 걸 먹고 싶은데?

give back

영영 to return something, often after it was borrowed; to work in a charitable manner for the good of the community

의미 1.빌려왔던 것을 돌려주다   2.사회 등에 환원하다

보충 give back 사이에는 sb나 sth이 올 수 있다.

1. I'll **give** it **back** to you after lunch. 점심 후에 줄게.
2. You took Chris away from me. You had better **give** him **back**.
크리스를 데려갔는데 다시 돌려주는게 좋아.

A: Why did you go to Martin's house? 왜 마틴의 집에 갔었어?

B: I had to **give** his jacket **back**. 걔 재킷을 돌려줘야했어.

pay back

영영 to give back money that was leant; to get revenge

의미 1.빌린 돈을 갚다, 상환하다   2.복수하다, 고통과 아픔을 갚아주다

보충 pay sb sth back …에게 …을 갚다

1. You need to **pay back** the money. 너는 그 돈을 갚아야 돼.
2. I need to **pay back** the credit card company.
카드사에 돈을 갚아야 돼.

A: Do you promise to **pay** me **back**? 돈 갚는다고 약속하는 거지?

B: You have my word. 내 약속할게.

put back

영영 to return something to the place it belongs
의미 1.다시 갖다 놓다   2.…을 뒤로 미루다, 연기하다

1. You just **put** it **back** where you found it. 발견한 자리에 도로 갖다 놔.
2. I need a minute to **put back** these items.
   이 물건들을 도로 갖다 놓는데 시간이 좀 필요해.

A: I borrowed Stacey's suitcase. 난 스테이시의 가방을 빌려왔어.
B: Make sure it's **put back** where it belongs. 원래 자리에 갖다 놓도록 해.

hold back

영영 to wait before doing something; to not permit something
의미 1.하려던 것을 연기하다   2.참다   3.…하는 것을 망설이다(hold back from ~ing)
보충 hold back (on) …을 연기하다, 참다

1. They told me to **hold back** from doing interviews.
   걔네들은 인터뷰하는 것을 자제하라고 했어.

2. You should **hold back** until you are calmer.
   넌 네가 더 침착해질 때까지 기다려야 돼.

A: Did you buy a new car? 새 차 뽑았어?
B: No, we decided to **hold back** on that. 아니, 우린 연기하기로 했어.

cut back

- **영영** to reduce the use of something
- **의미** 사용을 줄이다
- **보충** cut back on sth

1. They are either going to **cut back** on staff or give us a pay cut. 직원을 줄이든가 아니면 임금삭감이 있을거야.

2. They decided to **cut back** on fast food.
   걔네들은 패스트푸드를 줄이기로 했어.

A: I've been coughing all morning. 난 아침내내 기침을 했어.

B: You should **cut back** on cigarettes. 너 담배피는거 줄여야겠다.

---

get ~ back

- **영영** to have something returned to where it once was
- **의미** 자기가 갖고 있던 것을 다시 돌려받다
- **보충** want ~ back 돌려받기를 원하다

1. Do you **have** your cell phone **back**? 핸드폰 돌려받았어?

2. What makes you think I even **want** you **back**?
   왜 내가 네가 돌아오길 바란다고 생각해?

A: I left my book in the classroom. 교실에 책을 두고 왔어.

B: You need to **get** it **back**. 너 그거 가져와야겠다.

take ~ back

영영 to forcibly obtain and return something; to admit to saying something wrong or in error; to return an item to where it came from

의미 1.강제적으로 돌려받다, 돌려주다　2.말 잘못한 것을 인정하고 취소하다

보충 take it back 자기가 뱉은 말을 취소하다

1. Why don't you just **take** it **back** to where you got it?
   가져 온 곳으로 다시 돌려줘.

2. You can't **take it back.** You already said it.
   한번 뱉은 말은 취소할 수 없어. 이미 뱉었잖아.

A: I think this new coffee maker is broken.　이 새 커피메이커가 망가진 것 같아.

B: Yes, I'll **take** it **back** to the store.　어, 내가 가게로 다시 가져갈게.

come from

영영 to originate from a place or area; to be the birthplace or hometown of someone

의미 1.…에서 나오다　2.…의 출신이다, 원산지가 …이다

보충 Where과 come from은 합쳐져서 비유적으로 …의 원인이 되다라는 의미로도 쓰인다.

1. You think I'm ashamed of where I **come from**?
   넌 내가 내 출신을 부끄러워하는 것 같아?

2. Where does all this **come from**?　어떻게 하다 다 이렇게 된거야?

A: Where did this cake **come from**?　이 케익 어디서 났어?

B: I bought it at the new bakery on the corner.
   길 모퉁이에 새로 생긴 빵집에서 사왔어.

suffer from

영영 to endure the bad effects of a disease or illness

의미 심신의 병 혹은 안 좋은 일들로 고생하다, 시달리다, 고통받다

보충 suffer from serious pollution 심각한 오염에 시달리다

1. I don't want to **suffer** like that. 저런 고통을 맛보고 싶진 않아.

2. My notebook computer **has suffered** a lot of wear and tear.
   내 노트북은 많이 닳았어.

A: Does anyone in your family **suffer from** diabetes?
   가족 중에 당뇨병 걸린 사람이 있나요?

B: Yes, my mother had diabetes before she died.
   네, 어머님이 돌아가시기 전 당뇨병 이셨어요.

graduate from

영영 to complete all of the courses of a school and receive a degree

의미 졸업하다

보충 undergraduate 대학생, graduate 대졸자, graduate student 대학원생, graduate school 대학원

1. When did you **graduate from** high school?
   언제 고등학교를 졸업했니?

2. I really want to go to **graduate school**.
   정말이지 대학원에 진학하고 싶어.

A: When did you **graduate from** university? 대학교 언제 졸업했어요?

B: Quite some time ago! 꽤 오래됐어요!

keep~ from

> **영영** to have something remain secret; to not allow access to something
>
> **의미** 1.비밀로 하다 2. …하지 못하게 하다
>
> **보충** keep sb from ~ing …가 …를 못하게 하다, keep sth from sb …에게 …을 비밀로 하다

1. We must **keep** Diane **from** finding out the truth.
   우리는 다이안이 진실을 알아내지 못하게 해야 돼.

2. Kirk **keeps** everyone **from** coming to his house.
   커크는 모든 사람들이 자기 집에 오지 못하게 해

A: Why are there guards in the store? 가게에 왜 경비들이 있는거야?

B: They **keep** thieves **from** stealing things.
   그들은 도둑들이 도둑질을 못하게 하는거야.

result from

> **영영** to cause something because of an earlier action
>
> **의미** …이 원인이다

1. My depression **resulted from** the end of my marriage.
   결혼파탄 때문에 우울증이 생겼어.

2. These injuries **resulted from** your car crash.
   이 상처는 네 차가 부딪히면서 생긴거야.

A: Tina and her sister are very upset. 티나와 걔 언니는 매우 화났어.

B: The whole thing **resulted from** an argument.
   논쟁을 벌이다 그렇게 된거야.

look at

영영 to examine or inspect something visually

의미 1.쳐다보다 2.살펴보다

보충 Look at you!(애 좀 봐라!), 그리고 놀라운 것이 사물일 경우에는 Look at this[that]!이라고 하면 된다.

1. Leave it. I'll **look at** it if I get a chance. 거기 놔둬. 시간나면 볼게.
2. Don't **look at** me like that. 그런 식으로 날 쳐다보지마.

A: Patty is the most beautiful woman in the world.
   패티는 이 세상에서 제일 예뻐.
B: You seem happy when you **look at** her. 넌 걔를 볼 때 행복해 보여.

stay at

영영 to remain somewhere, usually for more than a day and sometimes for a long period

의미 하루이상 혹은 장기간 어떤 장소에 머물다

1. Can I **stay at** your apartment again tonight?
   오늘 밤 다시 네 집에 머물러도 돼?
2. Tonight I will **stay at** my place. 오늘 밤 난 집에 있을거야.

A: She doesn't have a place to live. 갠 살 집이 없어.
B: Maybe she can **stay at** a hotel. 호텔에 머물 수도 있잖아.

laugh at

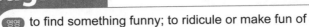

> **영영** to find something funny; to ridicule or make fun of
>
> **의미** 비웃다, 놀리다
>
> **보충** laugh at sb behind their back 뒷담화하다

1. He called me names. He **laughed at** me.
개가 내게 욕을 했어. 걘 나를 비웃었다고.

2. I couldn't stop **laughing at** your story.
네 얘기에 웃음을 멈출 수가 없었어.

A: People **were laughing at** my ugly shirt. 사람들이 내 후진 셔츠를 비웃었어.

B: You need to buy some nicer clothes. 넌 좀 괜찮은 옷을 사야 돼.

arrive at

> **영영** to reach a destination; to conclude or decide something
>
> **의미** 1.목적지에 도착하다 2.결론을 내리다
>
> **보충** 제 시간에 도착하다는 arrive on time, 예정보다 일찍 도착하다는 arrive ahead of schedule

1. When is he scheduled to **arrive at** the airport?
그 사람이 공항에 언제 도착할 예정이니?

2. Scientists **arrived at** this conclusion after much research.
과학자들은 많은 연구끝에 이런 결론에 다다렀어.

A: When is Tom scheduled to **arrive at** the office?
탐이 언제 사무실에 도착할 예정이니?

B: He's supposed to arrive tomorrow after 3 o'clock.
내일 3시 후에 도착하게 되어 있어.

be good at

> **영영** to have special talent or ability
> **의미** …을 잘하다(be great at)
> **보충** ↔ be not good at = be poor at = be terrible at

1. Kane **is good at** making money. 케인은 돈을 버는데 아주 유능해.
2. I'm **terrible at** making choices. 난 뭔가 고르는데는 젬병이야.

A: What do I do now? 나 이제 어떻게 하지?
B: You do what you**'re great at**. 네가 잘하는 것을 해봐.

jump at

> **영영** to accept an offer quickly; to spring toward something
> **의미** 1. 기회나 제의 등을 덥석 받아들이다 2. 포착하다
> **보충** jump at 다음에는 chance나 opportunity 등의 명사가 온다.

1. I **jumped at** the chance to go to Brazil.
   난 브라질에 가는 기회를 덥석 물었어.

2. They **jumped at** the opportunity to leave class early.
   걔네들은 단축수업할 기회를 덥석 물었어.

A: Tell them I will sell the house for $200,000.
   집은 20만 달러에 팔거라 그들에게 말해요.

B: I think they'll **jump at** the chance to buy it.
   그 집을 사기 위해 덥석 받아들일 것 같아요.

get at

영영 to influence or have access to something; to refer to the main point of something

의미 1. 영향을 주다 2. 접근하다 3. 도달하다 4. 핵심을 암시하다

1. I don't know what you **are getting at**. 무슨 말을 하려는 건지 모르겠어.

2. He began to understand what the boss **was getting at**.
갠 사장이 뭘 의도하는지 차츰 이해가 됐어.

A: Tom kept talking about his family. 탐은 계속해서 자기 가족얘기를 해.

B: Did you understand what he **was getting at**?
걔가 노리는게 뭔지 이해했어?

come at

영영 to move toward; to rush sb with the intent to fight or attack

의미 1. 도달하다, 접근하다 2. 위협하다

보충 come at sb 달려들다, 덤벼들다

1. Let's **come at** this a different way. What are his interests?
다른 방법으로 다가가자고. 걔의 관심이 뭐지?

2. I will **come at** you with everything I've got.
내 모든 것을 가지고 너한테 덤빌거야.

A: So your girlfriend said you were cheating?
네 여친이 네가 바람피고 있다고 말했다고?

B: She **came at** me with a lot of accusations.
여러 비난을 해대며 내게 덤볐어.

work at

영영 to make an attempt to improve or do better; to labor to finish a task

의미 얻으려고 혹은 향상시키려고 열심히 하다

보충 work at+일[~ing], work at a hotel(호텔에서 근무하다), work at nights(밤에 근무하다)와 구분.

1. I **worked at** getting the job done.
   난 이 일을 끝내는데 열심히 했어.

2. I tried my best to **work at** this marriage.
   이 결혼을 성사시키려고 최선을 다했어.

A: How do you like being a doctor? 의사가 된게 어때?

B: It's very difficult, but I'm **working at** it. 어렵지만 열심히 노력하고 있어.

Unit 06 around·through

away 떨어져, 사라지는	**ahead** 앞으로, 앞에
across 건너편에	**by** 옆에, …로
behind 뒤에, 뒤에서	**forward** 앞으로
towards …을 향하여	**together** 함께, 같이
through …을 통하여, …을 거쳐	
around …주위에	**against** …에 반하여
after …을 따라서, 향하여	
along …을 따라	
apart 떨어져, 분리	

run away

영영 to leave rapidly, often in fear; to leave secretly and illegally as a minor, often from a parent's home; to go out of control, as in the case of a vehicle or other machine

의미 1.급히 떠나다, 달아나다 2.가출하다 3.(기계) 고장나다

보충 run away from~ …에서 떠나다, run away with sb …와 함께 도망치다

1. You can't **run away** from your problems.
   넌 네 문제들로부터 도망쳐서는 안돼.

2. He **ran away** from home as a teenager. 걘 십대일 때 가출했어.

A: What would you do if you saw a ghost? 네가 유령을 본다면 어떻게 하겠어?

B: I'd **run away** as soon as possible. 가능한 빨리 달아나겠지.

walk away

영영 to quit or cancel something; to leave abruptly

의미 외면하고 그냥 가버리다

보충 walk away with sth …을 차지하다, 쉽게 이기다

1. Don't **walk away** while I'm talking. 내가 얘기하는 동안 가버리지마.

2. Did you think you could betray me and just **walk away?**
   날 배신하고 그냥 가버릴 수 있다고 생각했어?

A: The job is really easy to do. 그 일은 정말이지 하기 쉬웠어.

B: It doesn't make sense to just **walk away.** 그렇게 쉽게 해치우다니 말이 안돼.

get away

영영 to escape; to go on vacation; to leave someone alone

의미 1.도망가다 2.휴가가다 3.…을 홀로 남겨두다

보충 getaway n.휴가, Get away! 꺼져!, get away with it …하고도 벌받지 않다, 무사하다

1. I think we can **get away** before the cops come.
경찰이 오기 전에 도망갈 수 있을 것 같아.

2. Trust me, she'll never **get away with it.** 날 믿어. 걘 무사하지 못할거야.

A: I haven't seen you for a few days. 며칠간 너 보이지 않더라.

B: We were on **a get away** over the weekend. 주말동안 휴가갔었어.

pass away

영영 to die

의미 사망하다

보충 pass away at the age of fifty-five 55세에 돌아가시다

1. His wife is very ill, and will probably **pass away** soon.
그의 아내가 지금 위독한데, 아마도 곧 세상을 뜰 것 같아.

2. Did you hear that Johnny's grandmother **passed away?**
조니의 할머니가 돌아가셨다는 소식 들었어?

A: I can't believe the news about Nina's brother.
니나 오빠 소식이 믿기지 않아.

B: I know. He **passed away** at such an early age.
알아. 그렇게 젊은 나이에 가다니.

stay away from

- **영영** to remain apart, to not go near
- **의미** 1.멀리 떨어져 있다, 가까이 하지 않다, 접근하지 않다   2.관여하지 않다
- **보충** Stay away (from me)! 내게 다가오지마!

1. Mom told me to **stay away from** that guy.
   엄마는 저 남자를 멀리하라고 말하셨어.

2. **Stay away from** people who drink too much.
   술을 너무 마시는 사람을 멀리해.

A: Rachel is so beautiful. 레이첼은 정말 아름다워.

B: She's trouble. **Stay away from** her. 걔 골치덩어리야. 가까이 하지마.

keep~away from

- **영영** to prohibit contact with someone or something
- **의미** …가 …에 가까이 하지 못하게 하다, 멀리하게 하다

1. **Keep** the gas **away from** the fire. 가스는 불옆에 두지마.

2. **Keep** the kids **away from** the cookies.
   아이들이 쿠키에 손대지 못하게 해.

A: Jim says he's going to a bar tonight. 짐은 오늘 밤에 술집에 갈거래.

B: You better **keep** him **away from** alcohol. 걔가 술을 멀리하도록 해.

go ahead

영영 to get started with something; to take the lead; to get permission to start

의미 1. 시작하다, 시작하게 하다   2. 선두에 서다

보충 go ahead of sb …을 앞서가다, go ahead with~ …을 계속하다

1. **Go ahead** and open the e-mail. 어서 이메일을 열어봐.

2. **Go ahead** and start the party without me, Jane.
제인, 나 없이 파티를 시작해.

A: Please let me explain why I did that. 내가 왜 그랬는지 설명할게요.

B: I'm listening. **Go ahead,** but make it short. 어서 말해. 어서 말하는데 짧게 해.

get ahead

영영 to be successful, to achieve more than others

의미 앞서가다, 성공하다

보충 get ahead in the movie business 영화계에서 성공하다, get ahead of ourselves 너무 앞서가다

1. The best way to **get ahead** is through hard work.
성공하는데 가장 좋은 방법은 열심히 일하는거야.

2. Everyone dreams of **getting ahead** in life.
다들 인생에서 앞서가기를 꿈꿔.

A: Is there any way to **get ahead** at this company?
이 회사에서 성공할 무슨 방법이 있어?

B: You're going to have to work very hard. 넌 열심히 일해야 할거야.

come across

> **영영** to suddenly find something
> **의미** 우연히 만나다(come across sb), 우연히 찾다(come across sth)
> **보충** = run across = bump into

1. I hope to **come across** someone who can help me.
   날 도와줄 수 있는 누군가를 만나기를 바래.

2. He **came across** an old classmate of his.
   걘 같은 반에 다니던 오랜 친구와 우연히 마주쳤어.

A: Why do you visit antique stores? 왜 골동품점을 가는거야?

B: I hope to **come across** something nice. 뭐 멋진 것을 찾기바래는 맘에서.

stop by

> **영영** to visit a person or place in a short, informal way
> **의미** 다른 목적지에 가는 길에 잠깐 들르다
> **보충** = drop by, stop by to+V 혹은 stop by for sth

1. I'll **stop by** you on my way home. 집에 가는 길에 네게 들릴게.

2. I'll **come by** your office when I'm through.
   내가 끝나면 네 사무실에 들릴게.

A: Could you **stop by** at 5 o'clock today? 오늘 5시에 들릴 수 있어?

B: Sure, that time works for me. 물론. 난 괜찮아.

come by

영영 to visit a place casually; to obtain something

의미 1잠깐 들르다 2얻기 어려운 것을 얻다

보충 come by to+V …하기 위해 들르다

1. Good things are rare and hard to **come by.**
좋은 것들은 드물고 얻기가 어려워.

2. I **came by** to see if you could go out for dinner with me.
나랑 저녁먹을 수 있는지 확인하러 왔어.

A: This vase belonged to the emperor of China.
이 꽃병은 중국 황제의 것이었어.

B: Where did you **come by** something like that? 그런 것을 어떻게 구한거야?

get by

영영 to be able to survive; to be able to pass or move alongside

의미 충분하지는 않지만 겨우 버티고 살아가다, 최소한의 것으로 지내다

보충 get by on+돈 …로 그럭저럭 살아가다, get by with sth …으로 간신히 지내다[버티다]

1. You'll have to **get by** on little money.
너는 적은 돈으로 헤쳐나가야 될거야.

2. How did you **get by** without a job?
넌 직업도 없이 어떻게 버티고 살아간거야?

A: Why are you working as a laborer? 넌 왜 노동일을 하는거야?

B: I'm just doing this job to **get by.** 그럭저럭 헤쳐나가기 위해 이 일을 하는거야.

swing by

> 영영 to make a quick trip to see someone
> 의미 잠깐 들러서 …을 만나다

1. Can you swing by and get my report?
잠깐 들러서 내 레포트 가져갈테야?

2. I need to swing by my house to pick up my wallet.
난 집에 들러서 지갑을 가져와야 돼.

A: John was just admitted to the hospital. 존은 막 병원에 입원했어.

B: Let's swing by and see him tonight. 오늘밤에 잠깐 들러 걔 얼굴보자.

run ~ by

> 영영 to explain something to someone in order to get their opinion or approval
> 의미 의견을 듣기 위해 …에게 …을 설명하다(run sth by sb)
> 보충 Run that by me again 다시 한번 얘기해줘

1. Could you run the story by me? 그 얘기를 내게 다시 얘기해볼래?

2. I don't understand. Run that by me again. 이해가 안돼니 다시 말해봐.

A: It seems like it could be successful. 그게 성공할 수 있을 것 같아.

B: I'll run the proposal by the manager. 매니저와 그 제안을 상의해볼게.

Unit 01
Unit 02
Unit 03
Unit 04
Unit 05
Unit 06
Unit 07

go by

영영 to go to an area with a specific purpose; to use a certain informal name, especially a nickname

의미 1.특정한 목적으로 …에 가다   2.(닉네임) …으로 통하다

1. Let's **go by** and see if Angie is home.
   가서 앤지가 집에 있는지 확인하자.

2. His name is Timothy, but he **goes by** Tim.
   걔 이름은 티모시지만 팀으로 불려.

A: There's a large grocery store here. 여기에 대형식료품점이 있네.

B: Can we **go by** and pick up some food? 들러서 과일 좀 살까?

stand by

영영 to wait for further instructions; to fail to take any action; to be loyal to someone

의미 1.다음 지시가 있을 때까지 대기하다   2.아무런 조치도 못하다   3.지지하다, 편들다

1. She's the only one who **stood by** me in all this.
   걘 이 모든 일에 날 지지해준 유일한 사람이야.

2. All teams **stand by** and hold position.
   모든 팀은 대기하고 현위치를 고수하라.

A: It wasn't easy when she had cancer. 걔는 암에 걸렸을 때 쉽지 않았어.

B: Thankfully, her husband **stood by** her the whole time.
   다행히도 걔 남편이 내내 옆에서 지켰어.

put ~ behind

영영 to get over a bad or difficult experience; to move an object to the rear

의미 1.…을 뒤에 옮기다[두다]   2.나쁜 기억이나 상황 등을 잊다

1. I'd like to **put** my divorce **behind** me. 난 이혼은 잊어버리고 싶어.
2. I **put** the photos **behind** the counter. 난 카운터 뒤에 사진들을 놓았어.

A: It was a terrible accident. 그건 끔찍한 사고였어.

B: I hope they can **put** it **behind** them. 걔네들이 빨리 잊기를 바래.

fall behind

영영 to fail to keep up with others, to fail to meet an obligation; to drop out of sight in the rear of something

의미 뒤지다, 뒤쳐지다, 늦어지다

보충 fall behind sb …에 뒤지다. fall behind with~ 지불해야 될 돈을 지급 못하다, 늦어지다

1. Neil **fell behind** the other runners. 닐은 다른 주자들에 비해서 뒤쳐졌어.
2. I **have fallen behind** on my bills. 난 청구서를 내지 못하고 밀려있어.

A: How did you get lost overseas? 어떻게 해외에서 길을 잃었어?

B: I **fell behind** the people in my tour group.
내가 속한 관광그룹 사람들보다 뒤쳐졌어.

Unit 01
Unit 02
Unit 03
Unit 04
Unit 05
Unit 06
Unit 07

leave behind

영영 to surpass or do better than; to forget an item, to let something remain intentionally

의미 1. …을 놔둔 채로 가다 2. …을 훨씬 앞서다

보충 be[get] left behind 뒤처지다

1. **I left behind** a note for our hosts. 난 주인에게 메모를 남겼어.
2. **I left** it **behind** when I moved to Chicago.
   시카고로 이사갈 때 그걸 두고 갔어.

A: Have you seen my lipstick case? 내 립스틱 케이스 봤어?

B: I think it **was left behind** in the hotel. 호텔에 놔둔 것 같은데.

look forward to

영영 to be excited or happy about something that will happen in the future

의미 좋은 일이 빨리 다가오기를 기다리다

보충 look forward to+명사[~ing]

1. I'm really **looking forward to** Friday night. 금요일 밤이 기다려져.
2. **I look forward to** doing business with you in the future.
   언젠가 함께 일하게 되기를 바래.

A: I'm **looking forward to** getting to know you. 널 빨리 알게 되고 싶어.

B: Take it easy. We have a lot of time. 진정하라고. 우리 시간이 많잖아.

head towards

> **영영** to move in the direction of something
> **의미** …로 향하다

1. We're going to **head towards** home very soon.
우리는 곧 집으로 향할거야.

2. Carl **was heading towards** the bathroom.
칼은 화장실로 가고 있었어.

A: This concert is just about finished. 이 콘서트는 방금 끝났어.

B: I think we'll **head towards** the exit. 출구로 나가자.

put together

> **영영** to assemble; to prepare something, especially related to projects
> **의미** 1.함께 모으다 2.준비하다 3.종합, 편집하다 4.작성하다, 정리하다
> **보충** Put yourself together! 정신차려!

1. It took an hour to **put together** the puzzle.
퍼즐을 맞추는데 한 시간이 걸렸어.

2. We'll have to **put together** a proposal by the end of the week.
우린 이번 금요일까지 제안서를 짜야만 할거야.

A: Did you **put together** your wedding list? 결혼식 목록을 취합했어?

B: Not yet. I'm still working on it. 아직. 지금 하고 있어.

get together

영영 to unite with or join a person or group of people

의미 캐주얼하게 만나다(get together with sb), 만나서 …하다(get together and+V)

보충 get-together 만남, get yourself together 진정하다, 맘을 추스리다, get your act together 기운내다

1. Are we going to **get together** this weekend?
이번 주말에 우리 만날까?

2. I have to **get together with** my mother. It's her birthday.
엄마 만나야 돼. 엄마 생신이거든.

A: Well, it was nice talking to you. 얘기 나누어서 좋았어.

B: You too. Let's **get together** again soon. 나도 그래. 곧 다시 보자.

put ~ through

영영 to make someone endure something unpleasant; to put someone in contact with another person

의미 1.어려움을 겪게 하다 2.(전화) …에게 바꿔주다 3.학비를 대다

보충 put sb through to~ 전화를 …에게 바꿔주다

1. I'll **put** you **through** to someone in that department.
그 부서 직원에게 연결해 드리겠습니다.

2. Why do you **put** me **through** this? 왜 날 이렇게 힘들게 하는거야?

A: Jack keeps stalking me and calling every few minutes.
잭은 날 스토킹하며 계속해서 전화해대.

B: It's sad that he's **putting** you **through** hell.
걔가 널 끔찍히 힘들게 해서 안됐어.

be through

영영 to be finished; to have moved from one side to the other side

의미 1. 끝나다, 끝내다 2. 관계를 끝내다(be through with sb)

보충 be through with sb 관계를 끝내다, be through with sth 다 사용하다, 그만두다

1. **Forget it. I'm through** with you now. 신경쓰지마. 이제 너랑 끝났으니.

2. **I'm almost through** with the docs. 서류 정리 거의 다 끝나가.

A: I haven't seen Glenda and Art lately. 난 최근에 글렌다와 아트를 보지 못했어.

B: She told me their relationship **is through.**
얘가 그러는데 그들 사이가 끝났다고 그랬어.

go through

영영 to experience or endure something, to pass from one end to the other end

의미 1. 경험하다 2. 불쾌한 일을 견디다 3. 통과하다 4. 살펴보다

1. **Go through** the shopping center. You'll find one.
쇼핑센터를 통과해서 가시면 보일거예요.

2. It will take a long time to **go through** the files.
이 파일들을 검토하는데 많은 시간이 걸릴거야

A: I haven't seen Chris around lately. 최근에 크리스를 못 봤어.

B: He's **going through** a hard time and feels sad these days.
걘 어려운 시기를 겪고 있어 요즘 슬픔에 잠겨 있어.

get through

> **영영** to endure hardship, to survive; to reach someone by telephone
>
> **의미** 1.힘든 시기를 무사히 이겨내다 2.일을 끝마치다 3.통화하다, 연결되다
>
> **보충** get through (sth) 힘든 시기를 이겨내다, get through (to sb) …에게 전화로 연결되다, 이해시키다, get through with~ 끝마치다, 완성하다, 해치우다

1. We have to **get through** all the important stuff.
   우리는 중요한 일들을 끝마쳐야 돼.

2. What do I have to do to **get through to** you?
   내가 어떻게 해야 너를 이해시키겠니?

A: I'm not sure we can **get through** this difficult time.
   우리가 이 어려운 시기를 헤쳐나갈 수 있을지 모르겠어.

B: Don't worry. Things always turn out for the best.
   걱정마. 언제나 결과는 좋잖아.

come through

> **영영** to succeed, to survive difficulties; to grant or be approved
>
> **의미** 1.성공하다 2.어려움을 이겨내다, 극복하다 3.기대에 부응하다
>
> **보충** Coming through! 좀 지나갈게요!

1. Our approval didn't **come through**. 우리 승인이 안 났어요.

2. She will **come through** this. 걘 이겨낼거야.

A: The company still hasn't granted my request.
   회사는 내 요청을 아직 받아들이지 않았어.

B: I'm sure it will **come through** soon. 곧 승인이 날거라 확신해.

look through

영영 to gaze past something, as if it isn't there; to read or look at something quickly for information

의미 1.못본 척하다   2.빨리 훑어보다

1. When Gina saw me, she **looked** right **through** me.
   지나가 날 봤을 때 날 훑어봤어.

2. **Look through** those items and see if you want any of them.
   이 물건들 훑어보고 맘에 드는게 있는지 봐.

A: What happened after your store was robbed?
   네 가게 도둑맞은 다음 어땠어?

B: The cops had me **look through** some pictures of criminals.
   경찰이 몇몇 범죄자 사진을 훑어보게 했어.

run through

영영 to move rapidly into and beyond an area; to give a short summary of something

의미 1.빠르게 이동하다   2.대충 읽다

1. I **ran through** the intersection. 난 교차로를 가로질러 뛰었어.

2. Let's **run through** some of the proposals. 그 제안들 중 일부를 좀 보자.

A: There were a lot of new ideas at the meeting.
   회의에서 많은 새로운 아이디어가 나왔어.

B: Can you **run through** what was said? 어떤 것들인지 대충 말해줄래?

do without

영영 to manage or endure not having something

의미 …없이 지내다, …은 없어도 좋다

1. I don't know what I'd **do without** him.
   걔없이 어떻게 살지 모를 정도라니까.

2. What would you **do without** me? 나없으면 어떻게 할거야?

A: The grocery store didn't have any bread.
   그 식료품점에는 빵이 하나도 없었어.

B: We'll have to **do without** it for a day or two. 하루 이틀은 빵없이 지내야 돼.

look around

영영 to gaze in different directions; to compare various things

의미 1.주변이 뭐가 있나 둘러보다   2.…을 찾으려 하다

보충 look around+N …을 둘러보다, look around for~ …을 찾으려고 하다

1. Do you mind if I **take a look around** here?
   내가 여기 좀 둘러봐도 괜찮겠니?

2. Why **is** he **looking around** like that?
   왜 걘 저렇게 주변을 두리번거리는거야?

A: Can I help you with anything? 도와드릴까요?

B: No, thank you, I'm just **looking around**.
   고맙지만 괜찮아요. 그냥 구경만 하는 거예요.

hang around

> **영영** to stay in one place without doing much or any work
> **의미** 시간을 보내다, 어울리다
> **보충** hang around with sb ···와 어울리다, hang around+장소명사 ···에서 시간을 보내다

1. You shouldn't **hang around** people like that.
   그런 사람들과는 어울리지 말아라.

2. Why do you think Jim **is hanging around** the bathroom?
   왜 짐이 화장실에서 서성거리고 있어?

A: You shouldn't **hang around** people like that. 그런 사람들과 어울리면 안돼.

B: Why don't you just mind your own business? 네 일이나 신경쓰지 그래.

show around

> **영영** to guide others through a place they don't know
> **의미** 구경시켜 주다, 둘러보도록 안내하다

1. I'd be happy to **show** you **around** town. 기꺼이 시내 구경시켜줄게.

2. Let's say we get out of here. I'll **show** you **around**.
   자 여기서 나갈까. 내가 구경시켜줄게.

A: Let's go out. I'll **show** you **around** the city. 나가자. 이 도시를 구경시켜줄게.

B: That sounds like fun. 재미있겠는걸.

fool around

> **영영** to act silly, to play; to engage in sexual activity
> **의미** 1.빈둥거리다, 시간을 때우다   2.애인이나 배우자 몰래 섹스하다
> **보충** goof around, mess around

1. You can't **goof around** while you're here.
넌 여기 있는 동안 시간축내지마.

2. I **fooled around** with a girl on the staircase.
난 계단에서 여자애와 섹스를 했어.

A: Any idea why Lance was fired? 왜 랜스가 해고됐는지 알아?

B: I guess he got caught **fooling around**. 빈둥거리다가 걸린 것 같아.

get around

> **영영** to travel to various places; to know a lot of different people
> **의미** 1.이곳저곳 돌아다니다   2.소문이 퍼지다   3.다양한 사람을 알게 되다
> 4.어려운 문제를 해결하다
> **보충** V+around의 경우 이곳 저곳을 돌아다니듯 이사람 저사람과 성관계를 맺는 문란한 행위를 의미하는 경우가 많다. 여기 get around 역시 예외가 아니다.

1. New fashions **get around** on the Internet.
새로운 패션은 인터넷 상에서 빨리 퍼져.

2. There's no way to **get around** the rules. 이 규칙들을 피할 방법이 없어.

A: Seems like everyone became ill. 다들 아픈 것 같아.

B: The flu **got around** the whole school. 플루가 학교 전체에 퍼졌어.

turn around

영영 to reverse directions, to face the opposite direction; to improve

의미 1.몸을 돌려 …하다   2.방향을 바꾸다   3.상황이 호전되다, 호전시키다

1. **I turned around to see where it was coming from.**
   그게 어디서 왔는지 보기 위해 돌아섰어.

2. **You never know when things will turn around.**
   상황이 언제 돌변할지 아무도 몰라.

A: I can't see my brother anywhere.   내 형이 어디에도 보이지 않네.

B: If you **turn around,** you will see him.   돌아서면 있어.

come around

영영 to regain consciousness; to accept an idea or proposal after a period of uncertainty

의미 1.의식을 되찾다   2.결국 …에 동의하다   3.들르다

보충 come around to+장소/to[for]~ …에 들르다, come around (to doing~) 결국 (…하는데) 동의하다

1. **Just give her some time. She'll come around.**
   시간을 갖자고. 의식을 찾을거야.

2. **How come you never come around anymore?**
   왜 넌 더 이상 들르지 않는거야?

A: Brian was knocked out while boxing.   브라이언은 복싱중에 녹다운됐어.

B: Put some water on his face and he'll **come around.**
   얼굴에 물을 부으면 깨어날거야.

stick around

> 영영 to stay in a place without leaving
> 의미 가지 않고 남다, 머무르다
> 보충 = hang around = stay around

1. She didn't **stick around** to protect me. 걘 남아 날 보호하지 않았어.
2. We hoped you'd **stick around.** 우리는 네가 더 있기를 바랬는데.

A: You don't want me to **stick around**? 내가 옆에 있는게 싫구나?
B: I didn't say that. 난 그렇게 말하지 않았어.

run around

> 영영 to move rapidly through an area; to have numerous romantic partners at the same time; to be busy; to frustrate or annoy someone by giving them useless information (to be given the run around); to go places to talk or meet with various people
> 의미 1.뛰어 돌아다니다 2.바쁘다 3.동시에 여러 명을 사귀다 4.속이다(run around 핑계, 속임수)
> 보충 run around+ ~ing …하느라 바쁘다, run around with sb (남녀간) 바람피다

1. She's **running around** telling everyone that she's going to break up with Tom. 걘 탐과 헤어질거라고 말하면서 다녀.
2. I'm going to **run around** the entire park. 난 공원 전체를 뛰어다닐거야.

A: Sam says her husband has been unfaithful.
샘은 자기 남편이 바람을 피고 있다고 말해.
B: He **has always run around** on her.
그 남편은 항상 몰래 다른 여자를 만나고 다닌다니까.

walk around

> 영영 to stroll through an area, usually out of curiosity
>
> 의미 돌아다니다

1. I'm out **walking around** the neighborhood.
   난 나가서 집 주변을 돌아다니고 있어

2. We need to clear an area for people to **walk around.**
   사람들이 걸어다니는 공간을 비워둬야지.

A: Where are you going? 어디 가니?

B: I want to take a walk around the park. 공원 근처에 산책하러 가려고.

kick around

> 영영 to consider something before making a decision; to strike
> something multiple times with a foot
>
> 의미 1.결정에 앞서 검토하다   2.발로 걷어차다

1. Let's **kick around** some ideas before starting.
   시작하기전에 아이디어를 검토하자.

2. We **kicked around** an old soccer ball before starting the game. 경기시작전에 오래된 축구공을 살펴보자.

A: I heard you might get married in Paris. 파리에서 결혼할지도 모른다며.

B: It's just one of the ideas we're **kicking around.**
   검토하고 있는 생각중 하나야.

be against

> 영영 to be opposed to; to be right next to or leaning on something
>
> 의미 1.반대하다 2.…의 바로 옆에 있다 3.…을 기대고 있다
>
> 보충 be against the law 법을 위반하다, be against the rules 규칙을 위반하다

1. I'm against the plan. It seems like a bad idea.
난 그 계획에 절대 반대야. 안 좋은 생각같아.

2. You're telling me you're against the death penalty?
사형집행에 반대한다는거야?

A: Why are the students demonstrating? 왜 학생들이 시위를 하는거야?

B: They are against tuition increases. 걔네들은 등록금 인상에 반대하는거야.

go against

> 영영 to defy, to oppose a rule or code of behavior
>
> 의미 1.반대하다, 거슬리다 2.…에게 불리해지다
>
> 보충 주어로 어떤 결정(decision)이나 판단(judgment)이 와서, Sth go against sb 하게 되면 원했던 결과를 얻지 못했음을 뜻하게 된다. 즉 …에게 불리해지다라는 뜻이 된다.

1. This goes against her Catholic beliefs?
이게 걔의 카톨릭 신앙에 반하는 걸까?

2. Everything went against her. 걔에겐 모든 일이 안되었어.

A: My dad does not want me to become an engineer.
나의 아버지는 내가 엔지니어가 되는걸 원치 않으셔.

B: You shouldn't go against your parent's wishes.
부모님 바람에 거슬리지 마라.

look after

> **영영** to care for, to protect
> **의미** 1.챙겨주다, 돌보다　2.잘 관리하다, 책임지고 처리하다
> **보충** look after sb 돌보다, 보살피다. look after sth 잘 관리하다

1. Could you **look after** my pets for a while?
　잠시 내 애완동물들을 봐줄테야?

2. **Look after** the business until I get back. 내가 올 때까지 업무를 책임져.

A: Why are you staying home? 왜 집에 있는거야?

B: I have to **look after** my grandmother. 할머니를 돌봐야 돼.

be after

> **영영** to seek something specific; to occur following something else
> **의미** 1.…을 찾다　2.노리다

1. She **is only after** her husband's money. 걔는 남편의 돈만을 노려.

2. Mark **is after** someone to help him study.
　마크는 자기 공부를 도와줄 사람을 찾고 있어.

A: You've been preparing for the interview a long time.
　넌 오랫동안 면접을 준비해왔잖아.

B: I'm **after** a high paying job. 난 급여가 높은 직장을 구하고 있어.

take after

영영 to resemble someone else, usually used when a child resembles a parent

의미 (가족, 친척) 닮다

1. Do you **take after** your mom or dad?
   넌 아빠를 닮았어 아니면 엄마를 닮았어?

2. Little Sierra **takes after** her mother.
   어린 시에라는 자기 엄마를 빼닮았어.

A: Have you seen Charlie's little son? 너 찰리의 작은 아들봤어?

B: Yeah, he really **takes after** his father. 응. 아버지를 정말 빼닮았어.

inquire after

영영 to ask one person how another person is doing

의미 …가 잘 지내는지 안부를 묻다

1. Did anyone **inquire after** Laura's health?
   누구 로라의 건강에 대해 물어봤어?

2. He **was inquiring after** one of the girls.
   걔는 소녀들 중 한명에 대해 안부를 물었어.

A: Larry left before I got to the office. 래리는 내가 사무실에 도착하기 전에 나갔어.

B: He **inquired after** you when he was here. 그가 여기 있을 때 네 안부 물었어.

name after

영영 to give a newly born child the name of an older person, as a show of respect or honor

의미 …의 이름을 따서 이름짓다

1. **Were** you **named after** anyone in your family?
   네 가족들 중에서 이름을 따서 지었어?

2. Many boys **are named after** their father.
   많은 소년들은 자기 아버지 이름을 따라 지어.

A: Why is your son named Ralph? 왜 네 아들 이름을 랄프라고 지은거야?

B: I **named** him **after** my favorite uncle. 내가 좋아하는 삼촌 이름을 따서 지었어.

go along

영영 to join with others; to agree with or not oppose; to move smoothly and without problems

의미 1.함께 하다 2.동의하다(agree) 3.잘되고 있다 4.계속하다

보충 go along 잘 되어가다, 계속하다, 함께 가다, go along with 찬성하다 (agree)

1. Terry decided to **go along** with the plan.
   테리는 그 계획에 동의하기로 결정했어.

2. Just shut up and **go along** with things. 그만 입다물고 일들 계속해.

A: How is your computer business? 네 컴퓨터 사업 어때?

B: It's **going along** well. 잘 되고 있어.

Unit 01
Unit 02
Unit 03
Unit 04
Unit 05
Unit 06
Unit 07

come along

영영 to join a person or group; to be developing or advancing in a positive way

의미 1.함께 하다   2.잘 되어가다   3.진행되다

보충 = go along

1. **How does the project seem to be coming along?**
   프로젝트가 어떻게 진행되고 있는 것 같아?

2. **Do you want to come along?** 상대방에게 같이 갈래?

A: How is your search for a roommate going? 룸메이트 찾는 거 어떻게 돼가?

B: I think it's coming along well. 잘 되어갈 것 같아.

get along

영영 to enjoy the company of someone else without disagreements

의미 사이좋게 잘 지내다(get along well with sb)

보충 = get on with sb

1. **Do you get along with your mother?** 너 엄마와 잘 지내?

2. **My wife doesn't really get along well with most people.**
   내 아내는 대부분의 사람들과 정말 사이가 좋지 않아.

A: Do you get along well with your new partner? 네 새로운 파트너와 잘 지내?

B: I guess so, but I really don't know him very well yet.
   그렇지, 하지만 걘 아직 잘은 모르겠어.

tag along

영영 to join others when doing something

의미 함께 가다, 함께 하다, 따라가다

1. Do you mind if I **tag along**? 내가 따라가도 괜찮겠어?
2. She **tagged along** with her older sisters. 걔는 언니들을 따라왔어.

A: You went with the kids to the movie? 넌 아이들과 함께 영화보러갔어?
B: I **tagged along** to make sure everyone behaved.
   다들 얌전히 행동하도록 하기 위해 함께 따라갔어.

fall apart

영영 to deteriorate, to fail, to disintegrate, can refer to a physical object like a machine, and can also refer to the failure of things like negotiations

의미 1.조각조각 떨어져나가다   2.(신체, 정신) 무너지다

보충 I'm falling apart 너무 힘들어, My entire body is falling apart 몸 전체가 엉망이야

1. My life **is falling apart.** I have so many problems.
   내 인생이 엉망야. 문제가 너무 많아.

2. Our old car is beginning to **fall apart.**
   우리 오래된 차가 망가지기 시작하고 있어.

A: The old bridge is beginning to tip over. 오래된 다리가 넘어지기 시작하고 있어.
B: It's likely to **fall apart** soon. 곧 무너질 것 같은데.

tell apart

영영 to be able to see the differences between separate things, to see why things are not the same

의미 구별하다, 분간하다

1. I can't **tell** these different sodas **apart**.
   이 다른 탄산음료수들을 구분 못하겠어.

2. How can you **tell apart** the twins?
   그 쌍둥이를 어떻게 구분할 수 있는거야?

A: Mickey looks just like his brother. 미키는 자기 형과 비슷해.

B: They are so similar I can't **tell** them **apart**. 너무 비슷해서 구분을 못하겠어.

동사별 총정리

ask out   find out
belong to   hang out
blow up   put through
break up with   ⋮
come over   write down
drop by
fall for

accuse A of B 비난하다, 고소하다
act up 버릇없이 굴다, 고장나다
afford to …할 여력이 있다
agree to …에 찬성하다
agree with 동의하다, 찬성하다
apologize for 사과하다
apologize to …에게 사과하다
apply for 지원하다, 신청하다
apply to 지원하다, …와 관련이 있다, 적용되다
argue with 언쟁하다, 싸우다
arrive at 도착하다, 결론을 내리다

ask for 요청하다, 묻다, 물어보다
ask out 데이트신청하다
ask~ to 요청하다, 부탁하다

back down 잘못인정하다, 주장굽히다, 포기하다
back off 뒤로 물러서다, 진정하다
back up 지원하다, (컴퓨터) 백업하다, 후진하다, 뒤로 물러서다

be after …을 찾다, 노리다
be against 반대하다, …을 기대고 있다
be aware of …을 알고 있다
be busy with …으로 바쁘다
be done with …을 끝내다, 다 먹다, 헤어지다
be fed up with 질리다, 싫증나다
be finished with …을 끝내다, 마치다
be good at …을 잘하다
be hard on 모질게 대하다
be into 관심갖다, 푹 빠져있다

into

be on   전원이 켜져 있다, …을 책임지다

be over   끝나다, 끝내다, 방문하다

be proud of   …을 자랑스러워하다

be sick of   질리다

be supposed to   …하기로 되어 있다, …해야 한다

be through   끝나다, 관계를 끝내다

be tied up   꼼짝달싹 못하게 바쁘다

be up to   …하는 중이다, 꾸미다, …을 할 수 있다

be with   …와 함께 있다, 지지하다, …의 편이다

be worthy of   …할 가치가 있다

over

---

beg for   간청하다

believe in   …의 존재를 믿다, …가 맞다고 믿다

belong to   …의 것이다

black out   의식잃다, 정전되다

blame for   나무라다, 탓하다

---

blow out   불어 불끄다, 쉽게 이기다, 펑크나다, 큰파티를 열다

blow over   (어려움) 지나다, 폭풍이 잦아들다

blow up   파괴하다, 터트리다, 화내다

---

break down   고장나다, 신경쇠약해지다, 쉽게 설명하다

break in   불법침입하다, (구두) 길들이다, 새론 연장, 도구를 쓰다

break into   침입하다, …하기 시작하다, 새로운 분야에 뛰어들다

break off   관계를 끝내다, 본체로부터 떨어져나가다

break out   도망가다, (종기) 나다, 발발하다

break up with   헤어지다

---

bring about   야기시키다, 일으키다

bring back   돌려주다, 데려다주다, 기억나게 하다

bring in 가지고 오다, 영입하다, 도입하다
bring up 양육하다, 화제를 꺼내다, 컴퓨터화면에 띄우다

build up 강하게 만들다, 자신감을 제고하다
bump into 우연히 만나다
burn out 완전히 지치다

C

call back 다시 전화하다, 답신전화하다
call off 취소하다
call up 전화걸다, 컴퓨터 화면에 띄우다

calm down 진정하다, 진정되다
can't stand to …을 참을 수가 없다
can't wait to 몹시 …하고 싶어하다

care about 신경쓰다, 좋아하다
care for 돌보다, 좋아하다, 원하다

carry on 투덜대다, 계속하다, …을 지니다

catch on 이해가 빠르다, 유행하다
catch up with 따라잡다, 만나다, 새로운 소식 전해주다

cheat on 부정행위를 하다, 몰래 바람피다

check in 체크인하다, 확인하다, (SNS) 어디있는지 알리다
check in on 확인하다
check into 조사하다, 체크인하다
check on 조회하다, 확인하다
check out 확인하다, 체크아웃하다, 계산하다, 책빌리다

check over 철저히 조사하다, 확인하다
check with 물어보다, 확인하다

cheer up 기운나게 하다
chew out 호되게 꾸짖다, 야단치다
choose to …하기로 선택하다, 결정하다
clean up 청소하다, 돈을 많이 벌다
click on 전원을 켜다, 마우스를 클릭하여 열다
close down 가게 문 닫다, 폐쇄하다

come about 일어나다, 발생하다
come across 우연히 만나다
come along 함께 가다, 잘 되어가다, 진행되다
come around 의식을 되찾다, 동의하다, 들르다
come at 도달하다, 접근하다, 위협하다
come by 잠깐 들르다, 얻다
come close to …에 가까이 가다, 거의 …할 뻔하다
come down with 가벼운 병에 걸리다
come from …에서 나오다, …의 출신이다
come on 유혹하다
come out 나오다, 게이임을 밝히다
come over 가다, 들르다, (감정) 사로잡다
come through 성공하다, 극복하다, 기대에 부응하다
come to 도착하다, 총합이 …이 되다, 의식을 되찾다
come up against 직면하다, 대항하다
come up with 좋은 생각 혹은 변명 등을 생각해내다
come up 다가가다, 예기치 않은 일이 생기다, 다가오다

down

commit to 전념하다, 약속하다, 충실하다
complain about 불평하다, 항의하다

count on 의지하다, 기대다
count sb in 포함시키다

cover for 대신 일을 처리하다, 잘못을 덮어주다
cover up 은폐하다

crack down on 진압하다, 조치를 취하다
cut back 사용을 줄이다
cut down (on) 줄이다

D

deal with 처리하다, 감당하다
decide to …하기로 결정하다
deserve to …할 자격이 있다
die of …로 죽다
do with …을 어떻게 하다
do without …없이 지내다, …은 없어도 좋다
dress up 잘 차려입다

drop in 잠깐 들르다
drop off 차로 내려주다, 떨어트리다, 줄어들다
drop out 학교 등을 그만두다

E

eat out 외식하다
end up 결국에는 …하게 되다
engage in 특정한 행위를 하다
enroll in 수강하러 등록하다, 가입하다

F

fail to 실패하다, …하지 못하다, 고장나다

fall apart 조각조각 떨어져나가다, 무너지다

fall behind 뒤지다, 늦어지다

fall down 넘어지다, (옷) 흘러내리다

fall for 속아 넘어가다, 홀딱 반하다

fall in with 어울리다, 생각을 받아들이다

fall into …한 상태가 되다, 계획에 없던 일을 시작하다

fall on 넘어지다, 책임지다, 어려움 겪다, (기념일) 언제 …이다

fall over 바닥에 넘어지다

fall short of 기대치에 이르지 못하다, 달성못하다

into

---

feel free to 맘대로 …하다

figure out 이해하다, 해결책을 알아내다

file for 공식적으로 신청하다, 고소하다

---

fill in 서류작성을 하다, 세부사항을 말해주다, 대신 일봐주다

fill out 서류작성하다, 살이 찌다

fill up 가득 채우다

---

find out 정보 등을 알아내다

focus on 집중하다

fool around 시간때우다, 몰래 바람피다

forget about …을 잊다, 깜박잊다

forget to …할 것을 잊다

freak out 질겁하다, 화나다

G

get ~ back 돌려받다

get about 돌아다니다, 퍼지다

get ahead 앞서가다, 성공하다

get along 사이좋게 잘 지내다

get around 돌아다니다, 퍼지다, 해결하다

get at 영향주다, 접근하다, 도달하다, 핵심을 암시하다

Unit 01
Unit 02
Unit 03
Unit 04
Unit 05
Unit 06
Unit 07

get away   도망가다, 휴가하다, 홀로 남겨두다
get back to   되돌아가다, 다시 토의하다, 다시 연락하다
get by   최소한의 것으로 버티고 살아가다
get down to   도착하다, 내려가다, 노력기울이며 시작하다
get in touch with   연락을 취하다
get into   …하기 시작하다, …에 빠지다
get involved in   연루되다, 사귀다
get married to   …와 결혼하다
get off   (버스, 기차)내리다, 퇴근하다, 오르가즘에 오르다
get on   올라타다, (기차) 타다, 잘하다
get out   나가다
get over   이겨내다, 극복하다
get ready to   …할 준비가 되다
get through   이겨내다, 일을 마치다, 통화하다, 연결되다
get to   일을 시작하다, 화나게 하다, 도착하다
get together   만나다
get up   일어나다, 잠에서 깨다
get used to   …에 익숙하다, 적응하다
get worked up   흥분하다, 폭빠지다

give back   돌려주다, 환원하다
give in   포기하다, 제출하다
give out   정지하다, 배포하다, (빛) 발하다
give up   포기하다

go against   반대하다, …에게 불리해지다
go ahead   시작하다, 선두에 서다
go along   함께 가다, 동의하다, 잘 되고 있다
go by   …에 가다, (닉네임) …으로 통하다
go down   떨어지다, 내려가다

go for 좋아하다, (가격) …로 책정되다, …하러 가다

go in for 즐기다, 열중하다

go into …에 들어가다, 상세히 설명하다

through

go on 계속하다, 일어나다

go out 나가다, 외출하다, (전기)꺼지다

go over 검토하다, 좋아하다, …위로 가다, 반복하다

go through 경험하다, 불쾌한 일을 견디다, 통과하다, 살펴보다

go to (college) 학교에 진학하다

go to work 출근하다, 일을 시작하다

go up 올라가다, (수치) 오르다

go with …와 함께 하다, 포함되다, 어울리다, 선택하다

---

graduate from 졸업하다

---

grow on …가 좋아하기 시작하다

grow out of (습관) 그만두다, …에서 생기다, 커서 옷이 안맞다

grow up 성장하다, 자라서 …가 되다

H

hand in 제출하다

hand out 나눠주다, 정보를 건네다

hand over 건네주다, 책임을 전가하다

---

hang around 시간보내다, 어울리다

hang out 어울리다, 몸을 내밀다

hang up 전화를 끊다

---

happen to …에게 일어나다, 우연히 …하다

have to …해야 한다

have to do with …와 관련이 있다

head for 특정방향으로 가다

head towards …로 향하다

---

hear about …에 대한 소식을 듣다
hear of …의 소식을 듣다
hear out 끝까지 듣다

---

help ~ with 도와주다
help out 도와주다

---

hit it off 죽이 잘 맞다
hit on 갑자기 생각나다, 수작걸다
hit sb up 연락하다

---

hold back 연기하다, 참다, …하는 것을 망설이다
hold on 꽉잡다, 기다리다, 어려운 시기를 견디다
hold out 굴복하지 않다, 희망하다
hold up 지탱하다, 버티다, 강탈하다, 미루다

---

hook up with 소개시켜주다, 섹스하다
hurry up 서두르다

I

inform A of B …에게 …의 정보를 주다
inquire about 문의하다
inquire after 안부를 묻다
insist on 주장하다, 고집하다
invite over 초대하다

J

join in 함께 하다
jump at 덥석 물다, 포착하다

keep ~ from 비밀로 하다, …하지 못하게 하다
keep away from 가까이 하지 못하게 하다
keep in 억제하다, 감추다, 못나가게 하다
keep out 들여보내지 않다
keep up with 따라잡다, 연락하고 지내다, 잘 알다

away from

start

---

kick around 발로 걷어차다, 검토하다
kick off 행사 등을 시작하다
know about …에 대해 알고 있다
know of …에 대해 알고 있다

laugh at 비웃다, 놀리다
lay off 그만두다, 일시해고하다
learn to …하는 것을 배우다

---

leave behind …을 놔둔 채로 가다, …을 훨씬 앞서다
leave for 출발하다, (애인과) 헤어지다
leave out 제외하다, 밖에 두다

---

let down 실망시키다
lie to 거짓말하다
like to …하는 것을 좋아하다
link to 연결하다, 링크를 걸어놓다
listen to 듣다, 귀를 기울이다

---

live up 부응하다, 신나게 돈쓰며 살다
live with …와 함께 살다, 불쾌한 것을 참다, 견디다

---

log on to 인터넷에 접속하다

---

look after 챙겨주다, 돌보다, 책임지고 처리하다

look around 둘러보다, …을 찾으러 하다

look at 쳐다보다, 살펴보다

look down on 내려다보다, 경멸하다

look for 찾다, 구하다

look forward to …을 기다리다

look into 조사하다, 안을 자세히 보다

look out 조심하다

look over 검토하다, 살펴보다

look through 못본 척하다, 빨리 훑어보다

look up (정보)찾아보다, 방문하다, (상황)좋아지다

up

M

major in 전공하다

make a mess of 엉망으로 만들다, 망치다

make fun of 비웃다

make it to 제시간에 도착하다

make love to 사랑을 나누다

make out 이해하다, 알아보다, 성공하다, 애정행위

make up for 보상하다

make up 화장하다, 꾸며내다, 화해하다

mean to …하려고 하다, …할 생각이다

meet with 만나다, 우연히 만나다

mess up 망치다, 실수하다

mess with 간섭하다, 건드리다

miss out on 좋은 기회를 놓치다

mix up with 혼동하다

move on 다음 일을 하다, 다른 장소로 가다, 극복하다

move out 이사가다
move to 이사하다, 이동하다

name after …의 이름을 따서 이름짓다

occur to 갑자기 떠오르다
owe A to B …에게 빚지다

pass away 사망하다
pass on 죽다, 건네주다, 거절하다
pass out 졸도하다, 의식을 잃다
pass over 무시하다, 대신 …을 선택하다
pass up 기회를 놓치다, 거절하다

pay back 돈갚다, 복수하다
pay for 비용을 치르다
pay in cash 현금으로 계산하다
pay off 빚갚다, 보상받다, 성과를 내다, 뇌물주다

pick on 괴롭히다
pick out 선택하다, 제외시키다
pick up 픽업하다, 고르다, 사다, (상황)좋아지다

pin ~ on 책임을 전가하다, 고정시키다
piss off 열받게하다, 화나게 하다
plan on 기대하다, …할 생각이다
plan to …할 계획이다, …할 생각이다
point out 지적하다, 언급하다, 가리키다
prefer A to B …보다 …을 더 좋아하다
prepare for …할 준비를 하다

pull off   어려운 일을 해내다, 성공하다, 힘써서 떼어놓다

pull over   차를 길가에 대다

pull up   차를 세우다, 의자를 끌고 와 앉다

---

put back   다시 갖다 놓다, 연기하다

put down   기록하다, 내려놓다, 전화끊다, 진압하다, 비난하다

put in for   공식적으로 요청하다, 신청하다

put in   시간이나 노력을 기울이다

put off   연기하다, 혼란하게 하다'

put on   속이다, 무대에 올리다, 옷입다, 화장하다, 음악틀다

put together   함께 모으다, 준비하다, 작성하다, 정리하다

put up with   참다, 받아들이다

put ~ through   어려움을 겪게 하다, 전화를 바꿔주다, 학비대다

put ~ behind   뒤에 두다, 잊다

Ⓡ

remember to   …할 것을 기억하다

remind ~ of   …을 보니 …가 생각나다

reply to   응대하다, 답변하다

result from   …이 원인이다

rip off   훔치다, 바가지 씌우다

rob ~ of   훔치다

root for   (운동) 응원하다, 지지하다

---

run ~ by   의견을 듣기 위해 …에게 설명하다

run around   돌아다니다, 바쁘다, 동시에 여러명을 사귀다, 속이다

run away   급히 떠나다, 가출하다, 고장나다

run down   뛰어내려가다, 닳아지다, 특정 정보 찾아내다, 비난하다, 고장나다

run for   후보로 나서다, 급히 뛰어가다

run in (one's family)   집안 내력이다

run into   우연히 만나다

run off with   몰래 갖고 튀다, 눈맞아 도망치다
run short of   부족하다, 모자라다
run through   빠르게 이동하다, 대충 읽다

S

screw up   망치다
search for   찾다
see off   배웅하다
see out   (문밖에서) 배웅하다
sell out   다 팔다, 신념을 버리다

set out   시작하다, 물건을 밖에 두다
set up with   소개시켜주다
set up   준비하다, 설치하다, 일정 정하다, 누명씌우다

settle down   진정하다, 정착하다

show around   구경시켜주다
show off   자랑질하다, 과시하다
show up   모임 장소에 나오다, 당황하게 하다

shut off   멈추게 하다, 전원끄다
sign up for   들어가다, 가입하다
sit down   자리에 앉다
slow down   속도를 줄이다, 연기하다

sneak into   몰래 들어가다
sneak on   일러바치다, 몰래 다가가다
sneak out   몰래 빠져나가다

spend in   시간과 돈을 보내다

split up 헤어지다

stand by 대기하다, 지지하다
stand for 상징하다, 지원하다, 편들다
stand on …에 대한 특정한 입장을 갖다
stand out 두드러지다
stand up for 지지하다, 옹호하다

start for (경기) 선수교체하다, 시작하다
start up 시작하다, 창업하다

stay at 머물다
stay away from 가까이 하지 않다, 관여하지 않다
stay in 장시간 머물다, 어떤 상태를 계속 유지하다
stay out of 안좋은 일에 끼지 않다
stay over 머무르다, 외박하다
stay up 늦게까지 자지 않다
stay with …와 함께 머물다, …의 집에 묵다, 계속하다

step in 개입하다

stick around 머무르다
stick to …을 계속하다, 고수하다, 집중하다
stick up for 편들어주다, 옹호하다

stop by 잠깐 들르다
stop to …하기 위해 멈추다

stress out 스트레스를 주다
suffer from 고생하다, 시달리다

swing by 잠깐 들르다

tag along 함께 가다, 따라가다

take after 닮다
take care of 돌보다, 처리하다
take for 착각하다, 잘못알다
take in 섭취하다, 웃줄이다, 속이다, 집에 머물게 하다
take off 제거하다, 떠나다, 가다, 이륙하다, 쉬다, 옷벗다
take on 책임지다, 신규채용하다, 맞서다
take out 꺼내다, 데리고 나가다, 제거하다
take over 떠맡다, 인수하다
take part in 참여하다
take pride in 자부심을 느끼다
take sb out of 설득하여 …하지 못하게 하다
take up (시간.공간) 차지하다, 취미생활 시작하다
take ~ back 되찾다, 취소하다
take ~ to …을 …로 데리고 가다

out of

talk sb into 설득해서 …하게 하다
tap into 두드리다, 접근하다, 자료를 얻다
tell apart 구분하다

think about …에 대해 생각하다
think of 생각하다
think over 심사숙고하다

throw up 토하다, 집어치우다
tide ~ over 돕다, 당장은 …하기에 충분하다
trade for 교환하다, 바꾸다

try on 한번 입어보다

try to 해보다, 시도하다

---

turn around 몸을 돌려 …하다, 상황이 호전되다
turn down 거절하다, (소리) 줄이다, 밑으로 이동하다
turn in 제출하다, 잠자리에 들다
turn into …이 되다, 방향을 바꾸다
turn on 켜다, 성적으로 흥분되다
turn out 모습을 드러내다, 드러나다
turn up 나타나다, (TV소리) 키우다

around

---

tweet about 트윗을 보내다

U

used to 과거에 …하고 했었다

V

vote for 찬성투표하다, 제안하다

W

wait for 기다리다
wait on (식당) 시중들다, …을 기다리다

---

wake up 일어나다, 깨우다
walk around 돌아다니다
walk away 그냥 가버리다
watch out 주의하다, 조심하다
win out 이기다, 승리하다

---

work at 열심히하다
work for …에서 일하다, 효과가 있다
work in …에서 일하다
work on …의 일을 하다, 영향을 주다, 설득하다

work out 잘되다, 운동하다, 해결하다
worry about 걱정하다
would like to 지금 …하고 싶다
write down 기록하다, 적다

Unit 01
Unit 02
Unit 03
Unit 04
Unit 05
Unit 06
Unit 07

메모

메모

메모